KIDI
TREASURES

SOUTHERN SCOTLAND

Edited by Simon Harwin

First published in Great Britain in 2002 by
YOUNG WRITERS
Remus House,
Coltsfoot Drive,
Peterborough, PE2 9JX
Telephone (01733) 890066

All Rights Reserved

Copyright Contributors 2002

HB ISBN 0 75434 034 1
SB ISBN 0 75434 035 X

FOREWORD

This year, the Young Writers' Hidden Treasures competition proudly presents a showcase of the best poetic talent from over 72,000 up-and-coming writers nationwide.

Young Writers was established in 1991 and we are still successful, even in today's technologically-led world, in promoting and encouraging the reading and writing of poetry.

The thought, effort, imagination and hard work put into each poem impressed us all, and once again, the task of selecting poems was a difficult one, but nevertheless, an enjoyable experience.

We hope you are as pleased as we are with the final selection and that you and your family continue to be entertained with *Hidden Treasures Southern Scotland* for many years to come.

CONTENTS

Eastfield Primary School, Penicuik

Faye Marshall	87
Callum Runciman	87
Christopher Smith	88
Ansleigh Joyce	88
Andrew Ferguson	89
Jordan Grindlay	89
Eilidh Torrie	90
Heather Reid	90
Craig Devereux	91
Kevin Harrison	91
David Allen	92
Alexander Shreenan	92
Emily Kirkwood	93
Emma Ritchie	93
Paula Smith	94
Kyle Proctor	95
Amanda Smyth	95
David Robert Johnston	96
Rachel Wilson	96
Lauren McEwan	97
Marilyn McGrandle	97
Craig Winslow	98
Aimee Trainer	98

Longniddry Primary School, Longniddry

Rosie Smith	99
Joanna Keiller	99
Dale Gordon	100
Farren Brown	100
Calvin McDonald	101
Sophie Patterson	101
Lucy White	102
Lucy Simpson	102
David Sked	103
Jamie Greig	103
Rebecca Mitchell	104

Aidan Thomson	194
Kenneth Galbraith	194
Craig McKerral	195
Kerri McCorkindale	196
Matthew Hales	196
Fraser Cameron	197
Jennifer Galbraith	198
Karen Semple	198
Susan Houston	199

Stobhill Primary School, Gorebridge

Sindy Urban	199
Rachel Quinn	200
Amy Young	200
Loretta Flanagan	201
Danielle Robinson	202
Sarah Donaghy	202
Stewart Pearson	203

Strachur Primary School, Cairndow

Grant Gibson	203
Eilidh MacRaild	204
Tom Adrian	204
Elizabeth Pope	205
Iain-Hamish Paton	206
Zoe Hempleman	206
Hazel Hunter	207
Alistair Clark	207
Linda Robertson	208
Rory MacLachlan	208
Andrew Wilson	209
Naomi Sturrock	209
Laura Campbell	210
Katie McNair	210
Karin Reid	210

Toward Primary School, Dunoon

Troon Primary School, Trooon

The Poems

MY SCHOOL DAY

M y school is Blackburn Primary
Y ou are at my school.

S chool is the best ever
C ounting is what I like doing best at school
H ow busy we are for four and a half days
O ur teacher's name is Mrs Bulgin
O ur class is Primary 4/5
L istening to other people is one of the golden rules.

D o listen to the teacher!
A lot of people listen to their teacher!
Y ou must listen to other people.

Leigh Bridges (8)
Blackburn Primary School, Blackburn

POPPIES

P oppies are bright red
O n Flanders fields poppies would grow
P eople were injured during the wars
P eople died during the wars
I n every part of our land
E veryone was sad during the wars
S ome day peace will come!

Jade Macrae Springham (10)
Blackburn Primary School, Blackburn

MY SCHOOL DAY

M y teacher is a good teacher
Y ou are a very, very, good teacher.

S chool is fun
C an we play with the games?
O dd and even
O pen the door please!
L ook at the gym hall.

D o look after the classroom
A new boy came to our school
Y ou are good Mrs Bulgin!

Nicola Watson (9)
Blackburn Primary School, Blackburn

THE PLAYGROUND

I see the children playing with a ball
I hear the screams and shouts as they play
I touch the ball which I hold in my hand
I taste my place piece out in the playground
I smell the fresh air!
I wish I could join in!

Amanda McFarlane (9)
Blackburn Primary School, Blackburn

WIND AND RAIN

Yesterday the wind blew through the trees
It was more than just a gentle breeze.

Hundreds of people were blown away
It was a really terrible day!

Yesterday lots of trees were broken
And people's arms and legs were broken.

No one was pleased about the weather
Everything blew like a feather.

Umbrellas and hats were blown away
Yesterday was a terrible day!

Amy Clucas (8)
Blackburn Primary School, Blackburn

WINTER

I see the ice hanging from people's window ledges
I hear robins out in my back garden eating food
I smell the hot dinners being cooked
I touch the snow falling from the clouds
I taste the snow falling on my tongue
I wish I was near a fire now!

Elizabeth Edmonston (9)
Blackburn Primary School, Blackburn

PLAYGROUND

I see balls on the ground.
I hear people having fun.
I smell the fresh air.
I touch the playground toys.
I taste my crisps and sweets.
I wish we could stay outside all day.

Maclare Jamieson (9)
Blackburn Primary School, Blackburn

WINTER

I see frozen ponds
I hear the wind
I smell smoke
I touch snow
I wish I was warm and cosy
in my house.

Scott Begbie (10)
Blackburn Primary School, Blackburn

FOOTBALL

I went to the park
I got a ball
I got a lot of friends to play football
Before I played I went
Said 'Thanks' to my mum
Then we all had a big game of football.

Graham Grant (11)
Bridgend Primary School, Linlithgow

THE BIG BLACK BLOB

Is the universe a big black blob, sitting on its own,
or are there others out there too?
I believe, do you?

Is the universe really big, or is it really small?
Has light gone to the other side,
like a torch beam on a wall?

Is the universe a big black blob, expanding far and wide?
Will the universe ever end,
when the stars and things have died . . . ?

Mark Richmond (11)
Bridgend Primary School, Linlithgow

MY PIECE OF STRING

My piece of string
is a wonderful thing.
I can play with it.
I have lots of things to say about it,
my piece of string.

My piece of string
is nice and red,
it fits around my big bunk bed.

Lauren Baff (10)
Bridgend Primary School, Linlithgow

DO GET BETTER KATIE

Katie was going out to play
Her friends were out as well
They were on their bikes
Having so much fun
Then they went for lunch.

After lunch they went back out
And played hide and seek
Then they went to the pool
They came back at 5pm.

'Time for tea,' they said,
She said, 'Goodbye, I'll see you tomorrow.'
She had her favourite thing
She had a bath and went to bed.

In the night she woke up
She shouted, 'Mum, Dad, I don't feel well.'
She had to go to hospital,
Her friends found out the next day.

She wouldn't come out to play,
They both said, 'Ooh, do get better, Katie.
We hope you feel better,
We'll come and see you tomorrow.'

Kellie French (9)
Bridgend Primary School, Linlithgow

DOGS

Dogs short, dogs tall,
A dog's favourite toy is a ball,
Dogs fat, dogs thin,
A dog's favourite food out of a tin.

Dogs friendly, dogs fierce,
A dog has bitten ears,
Dogs sad, dogs happy,
Some dogs wear a nappy.

Becky Callachan (10)
Bridgend Primary School, Linlithgow

ON MY WAY TO SCHOOL

On my way to school today
I met a giant cat.
It said to me, 'Who are you?'
'Sammy,' I said and took off my hat.

'I have to go to school,' I said,
'Why? Why do you have to go to school?'
'I have to go to learn,' I said.
'But I like going in the swimming pool.'

Oh well I have to go,
I can't wait to tell my friends.
They probably won't believe me, though,
And that's how the poem ends.

Samantha Barrett (10)
Bridgend Primary School, Linlithgow

The Rabbit

One day while walking down the street
On the way to the supermarket to buy some meat
I saw something grey sticking out of the grass
With its rear end pointing to the sun in the sky
I walked over to it with extreme caution
And made sure not to frighten it away
With a shock it looked up, it was a rabbit
With a carrot in its mouth, chewing silently
I wanted to pat it on the back
But it went back into its burrow.

Ewan Murray (11)
Bridgend Primary School, Linlithgow

I Was Walking

I was walking by the burn
The heavy rain made the water churn.

Leaves and branches swam
Quickly past me on their way to the river and the open sea.

Lindsay Green (11)
Bridgend Primary School, Linlithgow

Winter

Winter is cold, very cold,
Icicles hanging from the roof,
And ice on the ground,
Where people slide and get hurt.

Liam McMeechan (10)
Bridgend Primary School, Linlithgow

WHAT IS THE GRASS?

The grass is green, oh so green.
You can see it everywhere you go.
It never leaves you
It always sees you.
Everyday you can water it.
You can stand on it.
It will never die.
Say hello, say goodbye.

Christopher Hamilton (10)
Bridgend Primary School, Linlithgow

LIFE

Life is just a great big tree,
That you have to climb,
When you get to the top,
The death bell chimes,
So you go to Heaven,
Or you drop to Hell.

Jamie Robb (10)
Bridgend Primary School, Linlithgow

THE TREE

Trees are green and brown,
They are good to have tree houses in.
You swing from a branch,
Then it snaps.
All you do is lie in the grass
Covered in branches.

Josh Hoggan (10)
Bridgend Primary School, Linlithgow

UNDER THE OCEAN

On a sunny Saturday morning,
I was under the ocean, scuba-diving.
I met a fish, it was silver,
It spoke to me and it said, 'Do you want to swim with me?'
I said, 'Yes, I will come with you.'
We swam in the blue ocean,
It went dark, it was weird.
The fish took me home on its back,
I fell fast asleep and woke in my own bed.

Kevin Mackay (11)
Bridgend Primary School, Linlithgow

THE BIG STORM!

The rain goes
splash, drip, onto the ground.
The wind
rushes through the air,
The lights
flicker, flacker.

The lightning flashes,
the thunder roars,
the wind whistles
through the tree branches.

The night is almost on us,
it's time for bed,
but I can't sleep.
All I hear is the
wind whistling, rain splashing,
lightning flashing and thunder roaring.

Andrea Grant (10)
Clachan Primary School, Tarbert

MY PET

My dog is large and furry!
As soon as you say, 'Going for a walk'
He's at the door in a hurry.
I wonder what language Spike talks.

Spike has got cute brown eyes,
He's lovely and cuddly.
I love the way he spreads out and lies,
But he can also be sly.

He loves to chew on bones and toys,
He eats his dinner in one minute flat.
Spike doesn't like being alone.
I know one thing for sure,
He loves chasing cats!
Yes that's my Spikey boy!

Keren Patterson (11)
Dalintober Primary School, Campbeltown

PARENTS

P   estering you all day long,
A   lways watching you,
R   emembering your first word,
E   nsuring you don't forget your lunch,
N   ot forgetting you're grounded,
T   elling you off for letting the dog in,
S   witching off the television.

Amy Muir (11)
Dalintober Primary School, Campbeltown

HIBS 2 RANGERS 0

I could hear half the crowd cheering,
The other half was fearing.
Zitelli was on, running at high speeds,
The Gers defence was desperately in need!

The penalty box came nearer and nearer,
His target became clearer and clearer,
David proved he was always a great kicker -
The ball went in then came out even quicker!

It was the second last minute of play,
All the Hibs fans were happy that day.
Luna came on and finished it off,
All the Gers fans went away in a huff!

Mark Good (11)
Dalintober Primary School, Campbeltown

THE FOREST

The green, green grass,
The green or brown trees,
Birds singing,
Clouds gathering in the sky,
Leaves gathering on the ground,
The deer and the creatures,
Peacefully talking in their own language,
Keeping the environment clear,
Unlike humans,
Who drop litter,
Who pollute the Earth.

David McGeachy (11)
Dalintober Primary School, Campbeltown

SMILE

This is a smile . . .
Something funny,
Really sweet,
From the people that you meet.

A passing joke,
Another smile,
Nothing is quite as nice,
As when you smile a happy smile.
Your heart is then at peace.

Róna Cameron (10)
Dalintober Primary School, Campbeltown

THOUGHT FOR THE DAY

If only I could be a football star,
I would get lots of money,
I'd buy a sports car.

I guess that's not what
I'm going to be,
Maybe I should concentrate on
Being just me.

Stewart McCallum (11)
Dalintober Primary School, Campbeltown

THE KEY FITS!

The key fits!
Trembling,
I turn the lock . . .
What could be inside?
Frightened,
I turn the lock further . . .
I can hear noises,
What are they?
Something could jump out at any minute.
I ask myself,
Still trembling with fear,
What could be inside?
Shaking with fear, I . . .
Push the door gently
And light
Shines through . . .
I push harder
And inside is . . .

Alix Brown (11)
Dalintober Primary School, Campbeltown

FEAR

F   oraging in the darkness,
E   erie silence,
A   nimal noises,
R   odents screeching.

John McCallum (11)
Dalintober Primary School, Campbeltown

YORKE FROM CORK

There was a young man called Dwight Yorke
Who played rugby football for Cork,
He gave a great shout,
When he was put out
And then he went home for some pork.

Graham Young (11)
Dalintober Primary School, Campbeltown

ROBOTS AND REPLICANTS

Robots and replicants
and clones too,
nobody cares,
not even you.
It's all in the future,
it's really going to happen,
not even you can stop it.

Boys and girls flying around,
hovercrafts and flying cars,
There might even be holidays on the moon,
You never know, it could happen.

Holograms and talking mirrors,
your teacher could even be one,
it's all in the future,
and it's going to happen
                soon!

Emma-Jane Eadie (11)
Dedridge Primary School, Livingston

HIDDEN TREASURE

My pup, Bengy, is a yellow lab,
he is very mad, never, never sad,
If anyone hurt him I'd give them a scab.
My dad said I made him mad.
Sometimes I call him my little lad,
I'm going to buy him a little tab.
I love my pup as much as my dad,
He makes me feel happy, not sad.
When I take a photo he looks like a white lab.
He's my best friend even though he's a lab.

My other friend is Ashley Wood, she is ten,
She loves her dog, it looks like a cute hen.
Ashley has more than one gel pen.
Ashley and I are as good as gold,
She always feels so, so, so cold.
I think she's shy, she needs to be told.
She's always wanted a golden lab,
Her dog has a bone as a tab,
On the bone there is something like a scab.

Hayley Black (10)
Eastertoun Primary School, Armadale

UFO

The stars and moon up in the sky,
Make me ask the question, why?
We think we're alone,
In this universe so vast,
The planets close to the Earth
Haven't been ventured past.

Those who think we're the only ones alive,
Out of all those planets, can't be wise,
Until we can go deeper,
We'll never know,
Unless you've seen a UFO.

Emma Carse (10)
Eastertoun Primary School, Armadale

HIDDEN TREASURE!

The most important thing to me,
Would have to be my dad.
He's really funny, bright and sunny,
and is never, ever, ever sad!
He's really cool, beats me at pool,
and tells me to stick in at school.

My wee brother Andrew Rodger
loves to eat a Jammie Dodger,
he can be really rather bugging
then again he's quite loving,
Andrew is really good at drawing,
like I said, he's still annoying.

Last of all I come to my mum,
her name is Lynn.
She's good at cooking meals for me
And also making me tea,
She's thirty-seven,
but thinks she's twenty-seven.

Stephanie Rodger (11)
Eastertoun Primary School, Armadale

HIDDEN TREASURE!

My little cat is black and white,
It lies on my bed and sleeps at night,
Its name is Poppy, oh so nice,
It brings in birds and also mice.

I got her from the RSPCA,
I was really happy on that day,
She was thin and sensitive, also scared,
I loved her and I really cared.

The first time I saw her
I was quite scared,
I could see her ribs,
Like they were almost bared.

One day she brought in a big crow,
She brought it in through the big window
And laid it on the carpet, so
I got a fright and shouted, 'Crow, crow, crow!'

I had two fish but she ate them,
Their names were Sharky and Splash'em,
I was shocked when my mum told me
They might be swimming in the sea.

This is a poem about my treasure,
My little cat who brings me pleasure.

Jordan Stevenson (11)
Eastertoun Primary School, Armadale

HIDDEN TREASURE

My family means the world to me,
I love them all so very much,
They are so nice, like sugar and spice
And do not eat any mice.

I have a little cousin who's two.
She likes drinking Irn Bru
She loves to laugh, she loves to joke
And she definitely does not smoke.

Kathryn Elder (11)
Eastertoun Primary School, Armadale

HIDDEN TREASURE

My little cousin is nearly two
He's very cute and looks up to you.

He definitely has loads of toys
And loads of friends (most are boys!)

Sometimes I think he needs a hutch
But to cuddle him, I love so much.

He's worth ten pieces of silver and gold
And I'll love him till I'm very old.

I wish he was the only cousin I had,
When he was born I was very glad.

Of him I am so very proud,
But sometimes he is very loud,
I'll love him till the day I die
And even then I will still cry!

Kirsty MacDonald (11)
Eastertoun Primary School, Armadale

MY CAT

My cat is really funny,
She will never stay in all day when it's sunny.

She'll go away
And stay out all day
And come back when it's black.

When I sit down beside her,
She is all warm and cuddly
Like a baby tiger!

But now she's in the autumn
Of her years,
Everything is cold and weird.

And that is my cat.

Stacy Johnston (10)
Eastertoun Primary School, Armadale

JUDY THE HORSE

Judy is fun,
Judy is great,
She loves to canter about all day,
She tries to nip,
But that's OK,
It does not hurt in any way.
She loves to jump fences and gates,
Judy and I are the best of mates.

Samantha Armstrong (10)
Eastertoun Primary School, Armadale

SUNSET

I see the lovely sunset in so many colours,
the shadow on the water of so many streams of fire,
the ducks flying high in the sky,
making noises as they pass by.

I hear the crashing of the waves,
I hear the talk of the people
sitting, watching in the sunset.

I feel the smooth breeze in my hair
and the trickles of water hitting my face.

I smell the salty sea water
and the smell of the evening wind.

Ian Brodie (11)
Eastertoun Primary School, Armadale

MY SUPER PARENTS

My parents are smart,
My parents are cool,
They are the best, I thank you,
My dad's super, he can make breakfast
Super fast.
My mum is brainy, she does my homework fast,
My parents are cool,
My parents are smart,
Oh Lord I thank you.

Clare Travers (9)
Eastertoun Primary School, Armadale

SUNSET

I see all the beautiful colours
mixing in the sea.

The sound of the seagulls in the daring sky
that really excites me.

The smell of the breeze in the dazzling fresh air
also the fish in the sea.

I can almost taste the seaweed underneath the shore
and some little fishes that I adore.

The touch of the sea so still and so calm
the touch of the sand so gritty on my palm.

Suzanne Hilson (11)
Eastertoun Primary School, Armadale

SUNSET

Sunsets are the most beautiful thing in the night sky.
Usually there's orange but in the summer sky
there are all sorts of colours.
Nice and beautiful, the clouds will float by
spreading all the colours across the sky,
especially for us to see and for us to go to bed.
Every night in the summer when the clouds are
soft and fluffy,
tuck up into bed as the light floats across the sky.

Lindsay O'Donnell (11)
Eastertoun Primary School, Armadale

HIDDEN TREASURE

My grandpas Bill and Joe have died,
But in my heart they're still alive,
I love them so, so very much,
Even though we are out of touch.
I also miss my budgie too,
And his cute little name was Loo.

When I went to scuba-dive
I met an ugly eel which was alive
He had bulgy eyes
And was a tremendously big size.

But my most precious treasure of all
Would be my little china doll
Which I got when I was very small.

Laura Brown (10)
Eastertoun Primary School, Armadale

SUNSET

I can see all the spectacular colours
and I can hear the swaying sea.
The sound of the gulls in the clear sky
it definitely cheers up me.

The smell of the air in the darkening night
it may be colourful but it is still light.
You can still hear children screaming and laughing
and the slow wind blowing.
As the sun is getting lower, the sea is still flowing.

Meghan Harris (11)
Eastertoun Primary School, Armadale

HIDDEN TREASURE

I love everyone in my family,
but my rabbit is rather special to me,
his name is Marble, small and furry,
he's so soft and funny, lovely and cuddly.

Even though he's dead right now,
my heart knows he's still around,
up in Heaven, looking down,
drinking wine and wearing a crown.

He was sometimes a little coward
and other times he was overpowered,
my wee cousin loved him too,
he sat all day and never grew.

I got him when he was very small,
I sometimes let him in the hall,
he'll always be my little treasure,
and I hope he has a lot of leisure.

Lindsey Patterson (11)
Eastertoun Primary School, Armadale

SAYING

My mum is always shouting,
'Nicole, get up,
Have your breakfast,
Brush those teeth,
Scrub them hard,
Brush your hair,
Or you'll be late!'

Nicole Fulton (10)
Eastertoun Primary School, Armadale

A Bird's-Eye View

As I look down I see Hadrian's Wall,
Like a large grey snake keeping
Out the enemies,
A long line of Romans standing guard.

The Roman road's like a big
Brown shoot,
With a large legend sliding
Down slowly.

A Roman fort defending
Hadrian's Wall,
A company of soldiers having a feast,
Gobbling their turkey and vegetables
Like they've never eaten before.

Emma Fulton (11)
Eastertoun Primary School, Armadale

One Day

One day at Loch Fay
I saw a very merry bay,
That day I was away
With my mama and
Papa and I like it.
Goodbye Loch Fay,
I'll come back someday.

Stephanie Wright (9)
Eastertoun Primary School, Armadale

SUNSET

I see spectacular colours,
Such as red, orange and gold.
The colours reflect off the sea
And it looks like a dragon's fiery breath.

I hear the sea smashing off the rocks
And the crickets chirping nearby.
There's also the sound of a bird's flapping wings,
As it flies off into the night.

I feel little sprays of cool water,
Touching my skin so gentle.
Accompanying it is a gentle breeze,
That blows my hair about.

I smell the salty water
And the suntan lotion from throughout the day.
All of these things happen,
When it is sunset.

Laura Macfarlane (11)
Eastertoun Primary School, Armadale

MY FAMILY

My name is Ashley,
Ashley likes Tom,
Tom likes Sally,
Sally likes Mum.
Mum does the hoovering,
Dad does too,
But I like Connor because he's new.

Ashley Syme (9)
Eastertoun Primary School, Armadale

A BIRD'S-EYE VIEW

A bird's-eye view of Britain,
Shows buildings, canals and castles
And Romans, Vikings and Saxons,
With evidence of battles.

First there is Stonehenge,
It was built on a plain,
A big circle of thin rocks,
Nobody will go there again.

Next there are the Roman baths,
With hot and cold for cleaning,
It's a place for relaxing
And to have a meeting.

Hadrian's Wall is on the border,
So enemies stay out,
It's a big stone barrier,
Enemies got past, I doubt.

Emma Harley (11)
Eastertoun Primary School, Armadale

SUNSET

S   un shines on the water like fire.
U   nder the sun is beautiful, calm water.
N   ever have I heard birds singing so nicely.
S   traight away I see the spectacular, bright colours.
E   very night you smell the air above the water.
T   he sky turns a dull blue after the sun goes down.

Scott Sinton (11)
Eastertoun Primary School, Armadale

A BIRD'S-EYE VIEW

A bird's-eye view of Britain,
How nice it is to see,
All the sights and statues,
Put there for you and me.

Roads that are so straight and thin,
Where soldiers walked, wearing tin,
They're so long, so big, so strong,
They could stretch to Hong Kong.

Stonehenge is a beautiful sight,
Tourists come at day and night,
It's still there, standing on the ground,
Like a circle it's shape is round and round.

The canals that flow are lovely too,
It's almost like a ribbon blue,
It flows like a water slide
And lands next to it,
Side by side.

Laura Dowds (11)
Eastertoun Primary School, Armadale

SUNSET

I see all the pretty colours going from one colour to the next
as the sun goes down.
I hear birds as they go home to bed when it gets darker.
I feel cold as the air gets cooler and begin to shiver by the sea.
I smell the salty sea and think of nice things before I go home
to end my day.

Lauren Sim (11)
Eastertoun Primary School, Armadale

SUNSET

I see the sun setting in the clouds
Behind the blue, snowy mountains.

I can hear the whistling of the stream,
Between the beautiful mountains
And the swaying of the trees.

I feel the soft, gentle breeze
Getting cooler and cooler
As the sun goes down.

I smell the dew of the bright green grass
Which sways in the wind.

No one's near, it's time to go home
So I'll say goodbye to the little gnome.

Mark Ferguson (11)
Eastertoun Primary School, Armadale

HIDDEN TREASURE

The most important thing to me is my teddy,
She is pink and very soft.
To play she is always ready,
She never goes up to the loft or down the stairs,
She never tells the secrets I share,
Because she's only a teddy bear.

My PlayStation is great,
I always stay up late,
Playing Harry Potter,
It's so good eating food
Whilst playing my favourite game.

Natalie Plant (10)
Eastertoun Primary School, Armadale

MY WEE SIS

When my wee sister was born I was all sad.
I thought that she would get all of the attention.
She got all the candy and toffees and lots of new clothes to wear
And all along I got nothing.
I felt like a hound stuck in a bucket.
One day it was raining and I was bored
But my wee sister had her rattle and toys.
She came over to me and said, 'Play, play, play.'
I played with her and her new toys
We played all the time till bedtime.
At night-time I read her a story to get her to sleep.
She is like an angel on a cloud when she sleeps at night.
When I am feeling sad she always cheers me up.
When I get in a row she hits me on the head
But the most important one is that she tells me
What is right and wrong.
That's my wee sis, Elise!

Nicole Moffat (10)
Eastertoun Primary School, Armadale

A TRUE FRIEND

My best friend is William Rodgers
I have known him since I was three
And when we slam doors and get caught
We bail each other out.
We always go to the Rangers games together
And sing our team on.
We are like twins
And will never be separated.

Greg Paterson (10)
Eastertoun Primary School, Armadale

AN UNUSUAL FRIEND

Mums and dads are always there,
they never let you down.
They always read you stories,
when you are going to bed.
They always buy you ice cream,
when you are sad.
Mums are soft and squishy,
they're like a trampoline,
they're like a first-aid kit,
always on the double.
Dads are like a pal,
mine's always in the gym
I think he's building a rocket ship
for me or fixing something.
Mum and Dad are always there
and they're my family.

Kirsten Mains (10)
Eastertoun Primary School, Armadale

MY BEST FRIEND

When I met him he was alright.
When I am in trouble he comes and helps.
We always have a laugh.
We almost do everything.
When I am in a fight,
If someone jumps in he does too.
We always bail each other out.
He is always there for me.
We always walk home together.
His name is Callum.

Scott Smith (10)
Eastertoun Primary School, Armadale

MY BESTEST FRIEND

My bestest friend is brown and furry
He is always there for me
I know he's only a teddy bear
But I've had him since I was three.

He is always there through thick and thin
And he cuddles into me
When something really sad has happened
He's always there for me.

He always sleeps with me
When troubles are near
I know I am ten years of age
I will never let him go.

When I am a hundred and three
And he is ninety-eight
Goldie, my favourite teddy bear
Will be here when I'm up there.

Louise Hunter (10)
Eastertoun Primary School, Armadale

A FRIEND

A friend is very cool
and he or she is never cruel.
A friend should make you laugh
and remind you to write a paragraph.
A friend is very loyal
and untangles you when you are in a coil.
Friends should be for life,
even if one is in London and the other
is in Fife.

Ross Drysdale (10)
Eastertoun Primary School, Armadale

MY BEST RABBITS

When I was five years old,
I got two rabbits called Snowy and Thumper.
Snowy was white and Thumper was black.
I hid Snowy and Thumper in my bed
But my mum always caught me.
I always loved them, day and night
But one tragic morning Thumper was dead.
We buried him in the back garden.
Three days later Snowy died,
We think she was too lonely.
We buried her too,
We put a rose on top of their coffin.

Callum McKinnon (10)
Eastertoun Primary School, Armadale

MY BEST LITTLE SISTER

When my little sister was born
She was small, like a bag of sugar.
She was sweet like candy
Every day we would play
Even when she was newborn.
When my mum was making the dinner
I would take my little sister.
When my little sister was born
I was nine years old.
Me and my little sister had our photo taken
I love her and every night we hug up tight.
When I am sad my little sister makes me laugh.

Natasha Little (10)
Eastertoun Primary School, Armadale

FRIENDS AND ENEMIES

Hayley is my best friend
She always laughs.
She was even laughing when she got her meningitis jab.
Natalie was my friend in P1/2,
But one day she was off.
Then I played with Hayley,
We became best friends.
Jade became friends with us,
Then I met Laura,
She was nice at first
But now we are enemies.
Then Lindsey became friends with Jade.
We all became friends at last.
Now Jade, Stacey and Lindsey are friends
And are always playing tig,
So Hayley and me went off and played somewhere else.
Then we fell out and Hayley went back but I didn't,
I got put in a different class from all my friends.
The only reason I stayed in it was because of my teacher,
Her name is Miss Lovell.
Nicole is always my partner at anything.
Michelle is my best friend in this class.
Hayley and me fell back in.
Hayley plays with me and Natalie,
So it starts all over again.
Tasca is my best friend in the world,
Tasca is my dog and she is very cute.

Ashley Wood (10)
Eastertoun Primary School, Armadale

MY FRIENDS

My friends are all there for me
As I am there for them.
We help each other every day
My friends sleep over and come to play.
My friends cheer me up when I am down
They always come around.
We laugh a lot and play all day
My friends are special in every way.
They stand by me through thick and thin
They laugh at every little thing.
We tell each other secrets
And never ever tell.
We do a lot together -
Isn't that what friends are for?

Nicola McLernon (10)
Eastertoun Primary School, Armadale

MY BEST MATES

My best mates are always there
We do almost anything.
We always stick up for each other
Or if we're in a fight and someone jumps in
My mates would jump in too.
When we get in trouble from the head
We bail each other out.
My mates sometimes have a laugh
My mates are always there for me
Like I am there for them.

Callum MacIntyre (10)
Eastertoun Primary School, Armadale

MY NUMBER ONE BRO

When my wee bro was born I was really pleased,
At last I had someone to play with.
He was a wee brother but I didn't care.
Sometimes he's good, sometimes he's bad
But I'm always there.
When he was five he was very brainy,
He helped me out in the hospital.
He made me laugh and told me secrets,
He gave me photos of me and him
And now I know I can trust him.
When I was being bad he stuck up for me,
When we went shopping he was very willing
And he bought me chocolate filling.
Who cares if we carry on,
I know we won't break our bond.
We will be loyal friends forever,
This is my number one bro, *Frazer.*

Craig Spence (10)
Eastertoun Primary School, Armadale

MY BEST DOG

When my best dog came to the house,
He was a one-year-old.

I got him when I was seven,
I won't forget him when I am a hundred.

My dog has big ears and he is brown and white,
He has a huge tail that waggles when the door knocks.

I care for him like he cares for me!

Grant Dickson (10)
Eastertoun Primary School, Armadale

My Cuddly Friend

My bestest friend cuddles into me at night
and his name is Grampa Bear.
He helps me sleep tight with all his might
and is always there with me.
He's very old but he's always new to me.
My teddy is older than me,
he is eleven and I am only ten.
We will always have our little den
under the covers with my friend.
That's the end of my poem
really just to say,
I will always take care of Grampa Bear
no matter what happens on the way.

Brianne Haddow (10)
Eastertoun Primary School, Armadale

My True Friend

Callum MacIntyre is a true friend indeed.
Callum and me will have an argument,
but in the end we are still best friends.
We do a lot together,
like going swimming, playing together,
building dens and going up the street.
If we are in trouble we will make up an excuse
or we will bash each other out.
Callum lives in my street
and we will just be true friends in the end.

David McKie (10)
Eastertoun Primary School, Armadale

THE BRAVE KNIGHT

It was a cool night
The cave was glowing bright
There was a brave knight
He was alone in the cave
But he was very brave
He saw a horse
It looked quite tame
He stole the horse
He found a princess
He gave her a kiss
She gave him a hiss
She turned into a snake
He took a break
He broke the window
He grabbed cake
He said, 'Better check,'
He ran away
He didn't want to stay.

Lauren Morrison (9)
Eastertoun Primary School, Armadale

HIDDEN TREASURE

I always wanted my own treasure,
I thought it would bring me lots of pleasure,
All the silver, rubies and gold,
I'd keep them till I was really old.

Then I remembered my mum and dad,
And how I love them and they love me back,
So I'm giving up the jewels, I've found a better treasure,
My family, the best jewels in the world ever.

Jade Drummond (10)
Eastertoun Primary School, Armadale

HIDDEN TREASURE

My dad is very good,
He buys me things that he should.
Toys, clothes, games and food,
and he looks like Robin Hood.

My hamster is called Jack
and he always looks sad.
The first day I got him,
I was very, very glad.

My PS2 is always good,
I play it through and through.
My most important things are my
dad and my hamster too.

John Cupples (11)
Eastertoun Primary School, Armadale

A BIRD'S-EYE VIEW

Below me I see a big circle of rocks on a lonely plain.
Below I can see a long snake keeping Scotland and England apart.
I can see big, straight, long, windy roads everywhere.
Below I see large manors all symmetrical, with lots of
windows staring at me.
Below I can see the big hill where the mines used to be.
Below I can see a factory with smoke and pollution.
Below I see a castle that looks dark and cold with a moat
around it.
Below I see a big, long cloud of steam.
I can see a big blue water slide.

Gary Goodfellow (11)
Eastertoun Primary School, Armadale

SUNSET

I see the reflection of the golden sunset bouncing off the sea.
I hear the seagulls and the gulls are laughing and singing happily to me.
I feel the cold breeze drifting by me, giving me the chills.
I smell the sea air coming into shore and seagulls eating rubbish,
pecking at it with their bills.

Craig Williamson (11)
Eastertoun Primary School, Armadale

ALIEN

A liens like to lie around
L iving creatures can be found
I n amongst the trees where no sound can be found
E ven if there is a sound
N othing can be found
          Remember, tiptoe around.

Sara-Jane Gibson (11)
Eastfield Primary School, Penicuik

LIMERICK

There once was a young man called Pete
Who liked to eat meat with his feet
After that he got fat
And looked like a rat
Now he can't eat with his feet!

Jodie Mullen (10)
Eastfield Primary School, Penicuik

BLUE

Blue is the colour of candyfloss
Blue is the colour of the sky on a hot summer's day
Blue is the colour of tinsel on a Christmas tree
Blue is the colour of my school jumper
Blue is the colour of fresh spring water
Blue is the colour of my pencil
Blue is the colour of ice cream
Blue is the colour of the deep blue sea.

Nicholas Duke (10)
Eastfield Primary School, Penicuik

ALIENS

A   liens come in different shapes and sizes,
L   ike us they have ears, eyes, lips but no hair,
I   wish I could meet an alien, and become friends with him,
E   arth is the planet they plan to roam,
N   ice aliens are small, and nasty aliens are big or tall,
S   aturn is their home and where they rest,
          but in my opinion aliens are the best.

Murray Gallacher (10)
Eastfield Primary School, Penicuik

GREEN

Green is for jelly that plays in my belly,
Green is for Celtic that wins on the telly,
Green is for lime that doesn't tell me the time,
Green is for an alien that really doesn't rhyme,
Green is for sauce that doesn't quite toss,
Green is the best it's no contest.

Conor McCormack (10)
Eastfield Primary School, Penicuik

GIRL'S PRAYER

Our Beanies, which art in bedroom
Hallow'd be their names
Thy TY come
Thy Beanies will be fun
In the shop, as it is at home
Give them this day, something to say
And forgive their appearance
As they appear before us
Give them this day, their TY say
And deliver them from shop
For the bedroom is their kingdom
The enjoyment at the story
Beanies forever and ever
        Amen.

Michelle Sclater (10)
Eastfield Primary School, Penicuik

BLUE

Blue keeps me calm
And is the colour of my jumper
Blue, blue, blue, wonderful blue
Blue football team
Blue curtains, blue bluebells
Blue, blue, blue, exciting blue
Blue is the colour of the cars
Blue is the colour of my best team
Rangers
Blue, blue, I adore you.

David Christie (11)
Eastfield Primary School, Penicuik

TELEVISION

Our TV that art in our bedrooms.
Hallow'd be thy picture.
Thy programmes come, thy programmes go.
In colour as it is in black and white.
Give us a day that good programmes come
And forgive the programmers
For showing too much football.

Lead us not into Teletubbies
Nor lead us into the Tweenies
For Sabrina is the greatest
The loveliest and the best
For TV and television,
    Amen.

Jodie McDougall (10)
Eastfield Primary School, Penicuik

THE BOY'S PRAYER

Our players who are in Tynecastle,
Hallow'd be the kirk,
Thy Hampden come, they will be Hearts,
On grass as it is on concrete.
Give us this day our Scottish Cup,
And give us good players as we gave them away,
Lead us not to first division but deliver us more money,
Ricardo Fuller stay with us, with your strength and your skills,
So get better and better so Levein won't give you away.

            Amen

Michael Park (10)
Eastfield Primary School, Penicuik

THE GIRL'S PRAYER

The shops which art in town,
New Look be thy name.
Thy clothes will come, thy will be gone
By the end of the day,
Cameron Toll where we are in Heaven,
Give us this day our daily shopping
And forgive us our shopping
As we forgive our shoppers.
Lead us not into debt to buy all the clothes,
For thine is the outfit, accessories and the handbags
Forever and ever,
Amen.

Janet MacDonald (10)
Eastfield Primary School, Penicuik

THE GIRL'S PRAYER

Our make-up which art on our faces,
Hallow'd be thy lipstick,
If I am going to a party, my eyelids will be done.
On our faces as it is on models,
Give us this day our latest eyeshadow colours,
Forgive the make-up makers for making it so expensive.
Lead us not into face masks and deliver us from spots,
For thine is the sparkly, silver nail polish,
Forever and ever,
    Amen.

Charlene McMahon (10)
Eastfield Primary School, Penicuik

MY PLAYSTATION PRAYER

My PlayStation what art in Heaven
Hallow'd be thy game
Thy Driver 2 will come, thy save will be done
On Game Boy as it is on PlayStation
Give us more games, to play at home,
And forgive our losses as we forgive our losers,
Lead us not into winning but deliver us from losing
For thine is the PlayStation the power and graphics
Forever and ever
    Amen.

Mark Ritchie (10)
Eastfield Primary School, Penicuik

BLUE

Blue is my colour, it is the best
Blue is the sky and the water
Rangers are blue, they are so good
The cars are blue and so are you
The blue scarves are blue
Blue. blue I love you

My jumper is blue and so is my room
My curtains are blue and so is my desk
I have loads of paper and blue toys
Blue, blue I love you.

Cameron Crawford (9)
Eastfield Primary School, Penicuik

BIRTHDAY

Our birthdays which are so great,
Presents they do come,
Thy cake is great thy candles blown out,
On tables and the plate.
Give us our sandwiches and our sausages,
And forgive us our greediness
As we gulp down the juice,
Lead us to the donkey and pin on the tail,
For parties are greatest and birthdays are the best.
Every year and every year
    Amen.

Lauren McLaren (10)
Eastfield Primary School, Penicuik

PURPLE

Purple is the colour of juice such as Ribena and Vimto,
Purple reminds me of blackcurrant sweets in my tummy tum,
Purple is the colour of the night sky, better go on tiptoe,
Purple is the colour of a Dairy Milk chocolate wrapper, yummy yum,
Purple is the colour of a hairband sitting on my friend's head,
Purple reminds me of lavender, how nice,
Purple pencils have purple-coloured lead,
Purple reminds me of a dice.

Zoë Robertson (10)
Eastfield Primary School, Penicuik

CHRISTMAS

C hildren going up to bed
H aving a sleepy head going to bed
R udolph pulling Santa on his sleigh in the midnight sky
I n the street snowmen being cold
S now on the rooftops
T hat's only Santa tumbling down the chimney
M y mum lets him back up the chimney
A s I run down the stairs Santa just leaves
S nowmen standing nice and still.

Aaron Parry (10)
Eastfield Primary School, Penicuik

GREEN

Green is the colour of grass, sprouts and peas,
It's also the colour of my mint ice cream.
Green is the colour of crisp packets and leaves.
Green is the colour of cars and seaweed.
Green aliens zooming round in outer space,
Green jelly is flying all over the place.
Green is the best, not red, orange or blue.
I think green's brilliant, now really, do you?

Lydia Keating (10)
Eastfield Primary School, Penicuik

A LIMERICK

There once was a young man called Pete
Who had very very very very smelly feet
He would not eat meat
Because of his smelly feet
And that is the story of Pete's feet.

Jamie Young (10)
Eastfield Primary School, Penicuik

THE ZOO

At the zoo,
At the zoo,
Smelly snakes snoring.
At the zoo,
At the zoo,
Enormous elephants eating.
At the zoo,
At the zoo,
Laughing lions leaping.
At the zoo,
At the zoo,
Terrifying tigers teasing.
At the zoo,
At the zoo,
Cute cats crying.
At the zoo,
At the zoo,
Wish I was at the zoo, the zoo.

Teri Gow (8)
Edinbarnet Primary School, Clydebank

SKY VIEW

Balloons, balloons in the sky
In the grass I lie
Watching the balloons with one eye
Balloons can go really fast while they last.

I've seen red balloons, green, blue and orange.
They look like buns in the sun.
I like them because they are fun.
I saw them with my friend Mo,
Under a special star that was seen from afar.

Bilge Morden (8)
Edinbarnet Primary School, Clydebank

CAT

In the dark a cat is coming
Sad and hungry and miaowing
Every night he comes here running
And really, really focusing.
He is focusing on a mouse
That has just come out of a house
Then . . . *pounce!* he caught the mouse
And ran with it into the house.

Stacy Morrison (8)
Edinbarnet Primary School, Clydebank

IT'S SNOWING ON BURNS DAY

It has not snowed this year at all
not in winter not in fall,
but at last the snow has come
and the fun has just begun.
Last night I watched the weather forecast
which gave me a fright.
She said it would snow,
she said the temperature would be low
but no, I did not believe her.
After school the next day
when I went out to play -

Hooray! Hooray!
It's snowing on Burns Day!

I got my friends I got my pals
we went ice skating on the canals.
We thought the fun would never end
with my pal and with my friend,
but soon it got too dark
we had to go home and leave the park.
When I woke up the next day
I was full of sadness and dismay
but when I went up to play
I thought -

Hooray! Hooray!
It snowed yesterday!

Stephanie Roden (8)
Falla Hill Primary School, Bathgate

SKINS

S   now-covered hills
I   n a wood
B   ears and wolves run
E   agles and hawks fly
R   ivers run cold
I   ce is not rare
A   nimals' cubs have fun
N   ight comes and more creatures appear

T   igers prowl through the woods
I   ts paws silently hit icy ground
G   rowl softly and there is a bang
E   verything runs away
R   ifles kill again
S   kins just for us.

Kate Stronach (10)
Inveraray Primary School, Inveraray

EVERY ANIMAL NEEDS A HOME

Every animal needs a home
No one wants to be alone
Don't cut down trees for your own sake
And leave the animals to live and play
Now we know there's not many left
Go on, be human, give poaching a rest
Even when times are tough
Remember life is hard enough
Every animal needs a home
Don't hurt them, leave them alone.

Emma Stark (11)
Inveraray Primary School, Inveraray

SAVE THE PANDA

The panda that I want to hug
Is being hunted by an ugly mug,
What has it done
To make it run?
Save the panda,
The panda, the panda.

The giant that is big and furry,
Please don't go in a hurry,
I want everyone to see you,
How cute and cuddly you are,
How cuddly you are.

Big, furry, black ears,
A big black nose,
I have thought of you in your home, eating bamboo.
Please don't go,
I didn't even get to see you.

Laura McMillan (10)
Inveraray Primary School, Inveraray

JUST LEAVE THE PANDA ALONE!

Pandas are like newspapers
They are black and white
So leave them alone!

Pandas like bamboo
They look nice and cute
So leave them alone!

Pandas are fluffy
They are friendly
So leave them alone!

Pandas are gentle
I love pandas
So leave them alone!

Vicky Lindsay (11)
Inveraray Primary School, Inveraray

PANDAS AND BAMBOO

Pandas sitting down, eating, playing, sleeping,
Never ever doubting.

Pandas like a bulb in a dark, dark room
Bang, pop! The light is gone.
What are we to do?

Playing, laughing, never wondering what is
Happening in the beautiful world.

Pandas like a bulb in a dark dark room,
Bang, pop! The light is gone.
What are we to do?

They're gone forever and ever,
You'll never see them again.

Danielle Webster (10)
Inveraray Primary School, Inveraray

I WANT TO SEE A PANDA

I want to see a panda
A great big cuddly panda
I want to go and see one by myself
I want to see a panda
A great big gentle panda
I want to go and see it on my own

I want to see a panda
A lovely cuddly panda
I want to go and care for it myself
I want to see a panda
I want to show how gentle and cute they are

I want to see a panda
Please stop hunting pandas
What have they ever done to hurt us?
I want to see a panda
I want to see a panda.

Gina Fyfe (11)
Inveraray Primary School, Inveraray

MONKEY'S POEM

A banana masher
A drum thumper
Thump down trees
Like you do to me
Chop chop chop!

Banana musher
Drum thumper
Loud growler
Knocking down trees
Chop chop chop!

Banana masher
Drum thumper
Loud growler
Hard fighter
Help us please!

Cassie Lindsay (11)
Inveraray Primary School, Inveraray

DOLPHIN CRIES

I hear,
But I can't see.
A sad crying sound,
They're crying for their
Lives and families.
They're crying for their homes
And their beautiful ocean world.

I hear,
But I can't see.
They are crying,
Crying,
Crying,
Crying,
Crying to stop destroying their homes.
They're dolphin cries.

Laura Peterson (10)
Inveraray Primary School, Inveraray

PANDA

He's a zoo pet, cute and cuddly.
He's a bamboo muncher
Or a black and white rug.

He's a soft cuddly toy,
He's a soft pillow
Being drove to extinction.

Allan Duff (9)
Inveraray Primary School, Inveraray

TIGER

T onight is hunting night
I t is very warm
G rowling everywhere
E verywhere there are men, better be careful
R ifle fires! I've been hit.

Jamie Divers (11)
Inveraray Primary School, Inveraray

THE ORANG-UTAN

Don't cut down the trees
Don't drain out the water
Don't cut down their homes
Don't kill the orang-utans.

Alasdair Munro (10)
Inveraray Primary School, Inveraray

TURTLE MAD

Cut down cruelty, the turtles are crying
Cut down cruelty, the turtles are trying
Cut down cruelty, the turtles are sighing
Cut down cruelty, the turtles are dying.

Rachel Maclean (10)
Inveraray Primary School, Inveraray

THE SWIRLING SEA

The blue waves are swirling,
The white horses are twirling
The sea crashes ashore
The aqua speckles pour,
The fish swim through the sea,
The long blue oceans free.

The waves crash along the sand,
Leaving a crystally foam band
The shells look like rubies
Sparkling on the shore.

The sun sets along the skyline
The oranges, purples and pinks look fine.
It gets lower and slowly sets,
The sun has gone to sleep,
Below the ocean deep.

Karen McFarlane (11)
Kilchoan Primary School, Acharacle

MYSTERY ON THE MOON

I went to the moon
Just the moon and me
I saw strange aliens, craters and spiders

It was very strange
Just the moon and me
I found some treasure
Oh, what glee
The lock was rusty
The key was there
Oh what heaven
Just look what's in there

Gold, pearls, necklaces, diamonds
I wonder what's next to it?
Urgh! Skeletons
Whose skeletons? I don't know
But I'm not here for long
Oh no!
I'm going back to Earth today
The skeletons and treasure will have to stay
Goodbye moon
Goodbye stars
My next trip will be to Mars.

Chloe Wilkie (8)
Kilchrenan Primary School, Taynuilt

A MYSTERY IN THE WOODS

Creeping and crawling through the woods.
Branches are snapping.
Leaves are falling.
Down, down, down.
A light starts to shimmer in the distance.
It gets nearer as we speak.
The mist starts to clear.
The light is now near.
Still creeping.
Still crawling.
It slowly gets darker.
The light slowly gets stronger.
A great big treasure chest with a yellow light beaming out.
Open the chest.
What's inside?
Sparkling pennies.
Diamond rings.
Gleaming pearls and glittery things.
Smiling in happiness.
Jumping with joy.
Laughing.
Giggling all the way home.

Jade Sutherland (9)
Kilchrenan Primary School, Taynuilt

MYSTERY OF THE DEEP

I am snorkelling in the ocean.
Riding through the waves.
Surfing the sea.
Diving further down.
Plunging into unknown mists.
Frightening figures sweep around me.
Slimy hands grab me and drag me away.
Trying to scream.
Only a large bubble escapes my lips.
Squirming and wriggling.
Escaping from my binding ropes.
Fleeing for my life.
I swim deeper.
The pressure intensifies and my fear grows.
Murky water surrounds me.
Queer and odd sounds fill my ears.
Something glistens immensely.
I swim even deeper.
Deprived of oxygen.
I hazily swim towards it.

Rebecca Eileen Reid (11)
Kilchrenan Primary School, Taynuilt

Hidden Treasure In The Jungle

I went into a creepy jungle.
There were snakes hissing,
Lions roared quite loudly,
There was a spooky old building in the jungle.
A cricketty old bridge lay ahead.
A smelly swamp with crocodiles sleeping,
In the swamp there were skeletons.

I fell down a huge hole.
There was a secret tunnel in the ground.
It was very dark.
A treasure chest was on the ground.
It was locked.
A key must be there somewhere.
There was a torch in my rucksack.
What was that shiny thing up ahead?
It was a key.
It was in a tree.
I got the key in the treasure chest.
Rubies, crystals and golden coins.

Niall Sinclair (9)
Kilchrenan Primary School, Taynuilt

TREASURE IN THE TOMB

I had come home from school.
It was late.
I had my dinner and went to bed.
I couldn't sleep.
I wished I could travel back in time.
I went outside on Saturday morning.
I built a time machine.
It worked.
I wrote the place I wanted to go.
It was Ancient Egypt.
I ended up in a strange town.
I saw the three pyramids of Giza.
I could just make out a secret tunnel.
It led into the Pharaoh's tomb.
I went into it.
I found some treasure and a mummy.
The mummy woke up.
I pulled a bandage and it turned to dust.
I dragged the treasure out and went home.

Calum Galbraith (8)
Kilchrenan Primary School, Taynuilt

RULES OF THE CLAN

To stay in our clan you must . . .

Wrestle a stranger
And fight for the chief
Fish for a trout
And shear the sheep
Wear a kilt and drive the cattle
Toss a caber and make it rattle.

Zaeem Ali (9)
Kinneil Primary School, Bo'ness

RULES OF THE CLAN MCDUFFY

To stay in our clan you must . . .

Track a deer
Without any fear
Hunt for rabbits
Without bad habits
Wrestle a stranger
When there's danger
Build a dike
Then go on a hike
Toss the caber
Better than your neighbour
Drive the cattle
And fight in a battle.

Liam Duffy (9)
Kinneil Primary School, Bo'ness

THE RULES OF THE CLAN MCME

To stay in our clan you must . . .

Hunt a rabbit - keep its nose
Shear a sheep right to its toes
Throw a hammer for a mile
Fight for the chief and never smile
Wrestle a stranger to the ground
Track a deer with the chief's hound
Toss the caber over a dike
Drive the cattle on a seven mile hike
Play the bagpipes, or a fiddle
And fish for trout while saying a riddle.

Russell Boyd Murdoch (9)
Kinneil Primary School, Bo'ness

RULES OF CLAN MCLEAN

To stay in our clan you must . . .

Harrow the ground
Without a sound
Do the Highland fling
Then loudly sing
Spin some wool
And keep the milk cool
Tell a tale
And make some ale
Bake the oatmeal
And dance a reel.

Robyn Lapsley (8)
Kinneil Primary School, Bo'ness

MY CLAN RULES

To stay in our clan you must . . .

Shear the sheep
But don't fall asleep
Do the sword dance
For the prince from France
Fish for trout
And bring it out
Wrestle a stranger
If in danger
And row over the loch
To Kirkintilloch.

Callum Wood (9)
Kinneil Primary School, Bo'ness

CLAN RULES

To stay in our clan you must . . .

Feed the hens
In their pens
Spin some wool
Onto a spool
Tell a story
Don't make it too gory
Milk the cow
Not the sow
Dye the cloth
And make the broth.

Jill Bow (9)
Kinneil Primary School, Bo'ness

THE NOISY CLASSROOM

It was so noisy that the football crowd
Couldn't hear themselves cheer.

There was so much racket that the Scottish
Parliament in Edinburgh couldn't hear their debates.

It was so noisy that Kinneil Band couldn't hear their playing.

The air-strike in Afghanistan was drowned out.

Kerry Rintoul (9)
Kinneil Primary School, Bo'ness

THE NOISY CLASSROOM

It was so noisy that my dog's ears
curled up in themselves.
There was so much racket that the windows
in the 'Learig' broke.
It was so noisy that the fairground
at Bo'ness Fair day was drowned out
and the flowers closed up their petals in fright.

Jacqueline Leslie (9)
Kinneil Primary School, Bo'ness

THE TREASURE

An old and ancient treasure map
Could lead to untold treasures
We'll follow the clues, the paths and trails
And through the dark corridors

We'll find the treasure
We'll celebrate with all our gold
If we can't find the treasure
We'll pull the place apart
We'll find the treasure definitely
There's the treasure over there at last!
We'll celebrate with all our gold.

Amanda McGrandle (11)
Knoxland Primary School, Dumbarton

THE CURSED TREASURE

Buried deep under the sand
There was a chest filled with treasure grand
Sitting in the darkness and waiting until
Some foolish old pirates come to unfill
But the pirates did not know that the treasure was cursed
The first thing that happened was that they had eternal thirst
The second was that they heard eternal thunder
The third was that they had eternal hunger
The fourth was the worst and most gruesome ever
They lost their lives and precious treasure
Back again in its tomb of darkness
Waiting . . . waiting . . . waiting.

David Jack (11)
Knoxland Primary School, Dumbarton

THE TREASURE

Long, long ago in Congo
some pirates tried to steal
A box of hidden treasure
The treasure hidden in a cave
Had been there for many a year
They sneaked into the cave
With torches lit
And searched for days
Until they found it.

Adam Cairns (11)
Knoxland Primary School, Dumbarton

A PIRATE'S LIFE

I'm a pirate
Fearless am I
We're going to find hidden treasure
And battle till we die

But we won't lose because
We're the toughest men around
We're tougher than the guard dogs
At the local pound

We'll read the map
Towards the treasure
We'll sail the seas
With pleasure

We arrived at the island
Safe and sound
We tied up the boat
And went to find

We found the treasure
Jewels and gold
Grabbed the money
As much as we could hold

We sailed back home
Proud to be
A pirate sailing
The Seven Seas.

Laura King (11)
Knoxland Primary School, Dumbarton

MOONSCAR'S TREASURE

Gold all around,
Dust on the ground,
Moonscar's treasure has been found,
Ghosts want revenge.

We better clear out,
Swords being drawn,
Heading for the door,
Arrows shot out.

Walls collapse all around,
Jump in cart, end of the line,
Duck, almost hit a beam,
Heading for the exit,
Safe!
Can't follow us now, home with treasure.

Steven McCubbin (11)
Knoxland Primary School, Dumbarton

HIDDEN TREASURE

Hidden treasure is many things
It could be a pirate's gold,
A king's jewel and crown,
A dog's bone or chewy toy
Or an infant's mother
Hidden treasure is many things
And many things more.

Andrew McWatt (11)
Knoxland Primary School, Dumbarton

SOMETHING MONEY CAN'T BUY

Once when I was having a nap,
I dreamt I found a treasure map.
On an island called the Isle of Wight,
In the middle of the night.

I dreamt I also found a cave,
Surrounded by lots of crashing waves.
As I spotted a small shadow coming near,
I began to shake with fear.

Suddenly I began to flee,
To try to run to a nearby tree.
Then something shiny caught my eye,
Something that money could not buy.

Suddenly someone called my name,
It was my mum to wake me up.
As my mum walked out of the room,
Something caught my eye,
It was the thing that money couldn't buy.

Samantha McLean (11)
Knoxland Primary School, Dumbarton

WHAT I DID FOR A LIVING

About a hundred years ago
We were on a ship going with the flow
We sailed the Seven Seas
We've heard many people's pleas
To keep their prized possession
Would be their only obsession.

But there is a day I remember
It was one cold night in December
We were on a hunt for treasure
We had a map with an exact measure
We were to look for gold
Which one day I will hold.

Matthew Brown (11)
Knoxland Primary School, Dumbarton

HIDDEN TREASURE

One day a long time ago
Pirates set off on a treasure hunt
The captain suggested so
So they left very early to leave for sea
And they were confident to find some
Hidden treasure

Later on that night a storm was building up
The captain had difficulties steering the ship
The waves were as vicious as a killer whale
That little ship was in an awful state
But the storm got worse as the night grew darker

Finally a couple of hours later
The storm died down
The captain suddenly saw a weird island
He shouted out with curiosity
'Full steam ahead to that island'

So they anchored at the island
They wandered around it until finally
They found the *hidden treasure!*

Craig White (11)
Knoxland Primary School, Dumbarton

THE HIDDEN TREASURES

Caves with traps and lots of rats,
It's a mystery to find this place,
Pirates and robbers searching for a map,
To find their way to richness and fame!

Along the beach they creep, creep, creep,
Tiptoeing all the way.
Don't move a muscle or you'll soon be caught,
Smuggling into the cave!

Keep a watch and a lookout too,
Searching for a hidden clue.
Imagine all that treasure to be found,
Crawling all over the ground!

Jane Cross (11)
Knoxland Primary School, Dumbarton

THE CURSED TREASURE

The cursed treasure was found long ago
And how we will never know
It happened one day in a land far away
On top of an old black book
Now this book, they say
Is about an ancient subway
Which sank down beneath the sand
So if you want to find this wonderful land
I suggest you go to find the following treasure
Where you'll seek your pleasure!

Pamela Miller (11)
Knoxland Primary School, Dumbarton

HIDDEN TREASURE

The mad pirate, sea-dogs,
Found treasure on the docks
And saw some women wearing frocks.

They loaded the treasure on the ship,
And then one pirate broke his hip.

The pirates sailed off to an island
They knew nobody would be there.
They buried the treasure in a cave.
Got back on the ship and gave it a wave.

They sat on the ship, smoking and drinking,
And doing a little bit of thinking,
About their next bit of thieving.

Steven Fernie (11)
Knoxland Primary School, Dumbarton

MY SISTER

My sister Gemma is tall and thin
She likes to play with her friends
She is enthusiastic and funny
She would love to have a pet bunny
She also plays hockey in her spare time
When her life is busy she gets dizzy.

Nicola Deigman (9)
Knoxland Primary School, Dumbarton

HIDDEN TREASURES

The grandfather - the grandfather's hidden treasure is
A bit of material, a scrap
From when his father was in the war
And when he never came back.

The grandmother - the grandmother's hidden treasure is
Her simple wedding ring, gold
And when she was poor and everything else went
It was the only thing she never sold.

The father - the father's hidden treasure is,
A wooden boat, a toy
It was a present from his grandfather
From when he was a boy.

The mother - the mother's hidden treasure is
A hairclip, emerald green
Her first ever present from her husband
It was the most lovely thing she'd ever seen.

The son - the son's hidden treasure is
A woollen bit of string
From the trainer that scored his first ever goal
The best ever thing.

The daughter - the daughter's hidden treasure is
A little cuddly toy
From when she was a little girl
It gave her so much joy.

The baby - the baby's hidden treasure is
A soggy rag doll
It's funny because when she first got it
She didn't care at all.

All these hidden treasures no one will ever know,
Not family, not friends, that's how it will be so.

Eilidh Hannah (11)
Knoxland Primary School, Dumbarton

ALIENS

I saw an alien last night
It was very big and bright
Short and shiny, all metallic
But not a pretty sight.

The spacecraft was wide
And very big inside
It scared me out of my mind
I just wanted to hide.

The door began to move
Very slow and smooth
And standing in the door
An alien, just off the floor.

He beckoned me in
His hands looked like tin
All shiny and bright
I picked myself up and ran away
Promising to come back another day.

David Clark (10)
Knoxland Primary School, Dumbarton

HIDDEN TREASURE

A hidden treasure is when somebody
Makes or gives you something
And you don't see them ever again.
You know to treasure it and keep it
As long as you can.
That is hidden treasure.

He means a lot to me.
He is my pa
And the thing that I am treasuring
Is a Mickey Mouse
He made out of wood.
When my nana's children did not have toys.

I have only seen once picture
But I don't know if it is him,
But I know he is a very nice man.
I really wish I could see him, but I can't.
He means so much to me.

My other papa gave me a Lion King watch.
He is very special to me.
I can remember what he looks like.

I miss all my papas and nanas.
My love is very very strong
And I try not to cry at night.

Joseph Kelly (11)
Knoxland Primary School, Dumbarton

MERMAIDS' TREASURE

Underneath the surface of the sea,
There is a special place
Where you can seek the most wonderful creatures
And see some beautiful faces.

These creatures are called mermaids,
Some say they don't exist
But I can tell you
That I have seen them, they do exist.

They hide this treasure so we can't snoop,
Some of us would be greedy, some would just look.
But they can't take any chances at all
Because of pirates, thieves and robbers who kill.

They are such caring creatures,
Strange they may seem, but underneath their delicate hearts,
They truly are so real!

Joanne McMillan (11)
Knoxland Primary School, Dumbarton

ONE FINE DAY

One fine day there was a jewel in the sea
One fine day there was some pirates at the bay
And one pirate said 'Get a pair of sea legs'
While looking for some clothes pegs
And someone shouted 'You big Ned go to bed
The only treasure you'll find
Is in yer head!'

Sean Lynch (11)
Knoxland Primary School, Dumbarton

HIDDEN TREASURES

My hidden treasure is the necklace my gran gave me,
It is very special because she is no longer here,
Lots of people have treasures like these,
That are very special to them too.

Some people have treasures inside them,
Like kindness,
Nobody can see this,
But it may surprise you who has this treasure.

Another treasure people can have is love,
What would the world be without love?
This is a great treasure to have,
But some people don't have this.

So treasures come in all shapes and sizes,
And some you cannot see,
But all treasures are special in one way or another.

Emma Ross (10)
Knoxland Primary School, Dumbarton

DIGGING FOR TREASURE

An old and ancient treasure map
Could lead to untold treasures
We'll follow the clues, the paths and trails
And find the place where they buried gold
We'll take our hammers, chisels and shovels
And now we will live our lives rich and fancy-free.

Vanessa Ferguson (11)
Knoxland Primary School, Dumbarton

HIDDEN TREASURES

A person's hidden treasure is love
That makes everybody happy and
Makes this world a good place to live in.

An animal's hidden treasure is its happiness
It makes everybody have happiness
When they see them running, roaring or hissing.

A porcelain doll's shiny, delicate china face
Is its hidden treasure of beauty and coldness.

A toy's hidden treasure is the way it
Makes people feel happy at Christmas time.

My hidden treasure is the way
I make my friends laugh
And the way I make myself feel happy.

Gemma Elaine Deigman (11)
Knoxland Primary School, Dumbarton

HIDDEN TREASURE

My hidden treasure is with me and will always be
It is with me, it will always be
While I live until I die
And when I go to Heaven
The only person I will tell is God
Because I can trust him to keep my treasure
He will not tell anybody as he is God
And is loved all over the world.

Ciaran Doherty (11)
Knoxland Primary School, Dumbarton

HIDDEN TREASURE

Stranded on a sandy beach,
Hidden treasure in a dark hole,
No one knows about it until one day . . .

The sound of the pirate's boat sound like a herd of elephants
Shouting and screaming.
They look for treasure like a spy,
They all go to the suspected place . . .
And start digging like the speed of lightning.

Hours and minutes later still digging,
Find a sparkle like a clown's eye,
They lift it up and find a chest full of gold,
They sneak to the ship like little mice,
They all cheer like a football match.

Back home sell beads, rings and bracelets to rich women,
Selling gold coins rapidly, they then become rich.

Every year they go back to the island,
Looking everywhere to see if there is any more,
But *fail*.

Alanna Jack (11)
Knoxland Primary School, Dumbarton

HIDDEN TREASURES

My hidden treasure is my grandpa,
I am wearing his ring to remind me of him,
For all the joy he gave me when I was young,
I know he still is with me inside my heart.
I will always remember him,
That's my grandpa.

My dad is my other treasure,
He gave me a hat and I will always remember that,
I found my dad after nine years,
I never knew him until now,
But I don't care what anyone says
I still love him,
That is my dad.

Steven Galloni (11)
Knoxland Primary School, Dumbarton

MY LITTLE BROTHER

I have a little brother
He is something of a bother
He likes toy cars
He says he is from Mars
When we are together
We are happy
And snappy
And never grumpy
His favourite animal is a seal
And I think he eats his meals
He's got golden hair
A cheeky smile
Some people think he's naughty
Well I don't care
Because he is my little brother
And I think he's funny
And better than golden money
I love him and he's my
Little brother.

Hannah Young (9)
Knoxland Primary School, Dumbarton

HIDDEN TREASURE

When people think of hidden treasure
They think of big brown chests
But I see something completely different
When I think of hidden treasure.

Hidden treasure can be jewels
Crystals, rubies too
Lots of people will agree
When they think of hidden treasure.

But if you take a closer look
Into a bad man's heart
You'll see that underneath the bad
There's lots of hidden treasure.

When I was a little girl
I thought of hidden treasure
As lots of jewels and lots of coins
That's what I thought of hidden treasure.

But now I am much older
It's very clear to me
There is some good in everyone
You've got to find the hidden treasure.

Carolyn Bell (11)
Knoxland Primary School, Dumbarton

TREASURE HUNT

Five hundred years ago
I was walking in the snow
Let alone did we know
There was treasure in the snow

So I'm walking in the snow
Then I fell through a hole
Falling and falling through a tunnel in the snow
Then it stops, quiet, I smacked my head on a pole.

Kristofer Miller (11)
Knoxland Primary School, Dumbarton

MY DEEPEST DESIRE

There is something about my deepest desire
That no one could possibly buy
I wish I could possibly get it
But my mum won't even try

I will tell you what I really want
But you better not tell my mum
What I really, really want
Is a new dog

I'll call him Buster
I'll feed him Pedigree Chum
I'll take him for walks through the park
Please Mum, get us a dog?

I wish I could get a dog
But I've got more chance of getting a frog
My auntie came on Saturday
And asked me, 'What do you want for your birthday?'
I said, 'Can I have a dog?'
My auntie said, 'I'll have to ask your mum.'
I have no chance of getting a dog.

Grant MacLean (9)
Knoxland Primary School, Dumbarton

GRANNY SEWING

Granny
Sewing is a
lovely, cheery and
jolly
person
But when
she
goes to
do
some
sewing
she always
takes
a
moody boots
I
wonder
I
wonder
why, why, why
Next time she should take
an
angry tablet.

Rebecca McLaughlin (9)
Knoxland Primary School, Dumbarton

HIDDEN TREASURE

Hidden treasure is like a locked up jewel,
Deep inside a castle dungeon,
Just waiting to be set free.

Hidden treasure is like a competition prize,
Hidden away in its sachet,
Just waiting to be opened.

Hidden treasure is like an concealed passion for someone,
A complete secret,
Just waiting to be told.

Hidden treasure is anything you want it to be,
Anything you feel strongly about,
Anything you feel is special - anything at all.

David Wiggins (11)
Knoxland Primary School, Dumbarton

SCHOOL

I go to school five times a week
At play time we play hide and seek,
I also eat my yummy snack
While I hide behind someone's back.

My favourite subject is drawing art,
With that I always hit the mark,
My biggest weakness is mostly maths
If it's a fraction question I always pass.

When it's time to eat my lunch
The café has nice things to munch,
Chips are my favourite thing on the list,
I always find them hard to resist.

When we're writing,
No one's fighting,
It's always very nice
When we're quiet as mice.

I like going home, especially best,
When the bell rings, I always beat the rest!

Jay Bloomfield (10)
Knoxland Primary School, Dumbarton

HIDDEN TREASURE

I got a letter about hidden treasure,
It was signed Anon!
It showed a map,
Down by the loch.
I set out to find my treasure.

By the water I saw a cave.
I got to the cave
And looked inside this dark, dark wonder.
I stopped and thought . . . then I wandered in.

I walked in, getting deeper and deeper,
The water at my knees!
Finally there was something shining,
I found it!
It was my treasure.

Melissa Dunn (11)
Knoxland Primary School, Dumbarton

HIDDEN TREASURE

A hidden treasure is friendship.
Friendship is like a soft breeze of air on a sunny day.
Friendship is as sweet as sugar ready to be mixed with a cup of tea.
Friendship is a beam of light on a dark and dull day.
A hidden treasure is an uncut diamond washed up by the sea.
An uncut diamond is a present to a love that shall not be.
A hidden treasure is a pen from a grandpa you'll never see.
My hidden treasure is love.

Emma Hawthorn (11)
Knoxland Primary School, Dumbarton

KITTIE CAT KITTEN

Kittie cat kitten
   plays in the snow
Kittie cat kitten
   has a bow
Kittie cat kitten
   hates bad weather
Kittie cat kitten
   loves her bed so

Kittie cat kitten
   is my special friend
Kittie cat kitten
   drives me round the bend
Kittie cat kitten
   is a cheeky little thing
While the telephone goes
   bring, bring, bring!

Faye Marshall (9)
Knoxland Primary School, Dumbarton

CHILDREN OF THE WEEK

Monday's child makes mistakes
Tuesday's child examines lakes
Wednesday's child is extremely funny
Thursday's child is like a bunny
Friday's child has chubby knees
Saturday's child hates broccoli and peas
But Sunday's child fits in any of these.

Callum Runciman (9)
Knoxland Primary School, Dumbarton

HIDDEN TREASURE

A hidden treasure is a watch passed down from several generations,
Found on a beach in Argentina in 1864,
Gone from father to son,
This is a treasure to me.

Hidden treasure is gold doubloons in a chest
Buried in the sand, hundreds of miles deep,
Several people died of starvation in the race to find it.

A hidden treasure is a feeling deep inside the body,
Not expressed in many years,
Then suddenly an explosion of emotion.

Hidden treasure has a great power on many people,
Hidden treasure can be from a button to a pen,
I have a hidden treasure . . . do you?

Christopher Smith (11)
Knoxland Primary School, Dumbarton

SUNNY SUNDAY

I do not like the weather
It is always windy, rainy and never sunny.

I wake up on Monday morning it is windy
On Tuesday it is stormy
On Wednesday it is rainy
On Thursday it is windy again
On Friday it is rainy again
On Saturday it is stormy again
And finally on Sunday it is *sunny.*

Ansleigh Joyce (9)
Knoxland Primary School, Dumbarton

HIDDEN TREASURES

A hidden treasure is digging a hole and finding jewels and gold
That a pirate buried during a war.
Opening up the chest the sound of the creaking
Is like a cockroach at night.
The giant box is finally open
Taking all of my strength out of my body.
I was exhausted from opening the box
I felt like I'd just ran a marathon!
I was shocked when I looked in
My jaw could have fallen off.
In the chest was a blinding sight of
Gold and silver coins with sparkling jewels.

Andrew Ferguson (11)
Knoxland Primary School, Dumbarton

HIDDEN TREASURE

Hidden in the sea below,
A chest full of all the treasures you know.
Full of sparkling rubies that gleam like a star
And diamonds that shine like a brand new car.

There's gold bars as big as bowling balls,
Rolexes, 24 carat gold and solid gold dolls.
Luck luckier than a silver horseshoe
And all the things are renewed.

But the best treasure of all is love,
That's all this sea dog is after.

Jordan Grindlay (11)
Knoxland Primary School, Dumbarton

JAYNE

Jayne is my little sister, she's noisy and fast
But she's not fast enough for me!
She always hides or sneaks up on you
She can be very annoying and irritating
She always blames me for
The fingerprints in the chocolate cake
The paint on the sink
Dirty towels
Broken toys
Lipstick on the bunk beds and the mirror
I say she can't do anything
She gets annoyed at that
I say she's the Devil
And mum says that I'm her angel
So that's what I really like about Jayne
She makes *me* look good!

Eilidh Torrie (9)
Knoxland Primary School, Dumbarton

MR CLOUD

Mr Cloud lives in the sky
And Mr Cloud likes steak pie
Mr Cloud and his wife Penelope sit in the clouds talking away
To their children Faye and Jay
Faye is the youngest, small and divine
I think Faye is just fine
As for Jay, troublemaker too
Annoying her sister Faye
And I think she is horrible and scary
My favourite is Faye, my best of all friend
And our friendship will never end.

Heather Reid (9)
Knoxland Primary School, Dumbarton

YASMINE

Yasmine is my little sister
She is very active
She can be very annoying
And always bugging me

Yasmine never takes the blame
She always blames it on me
Then I get into trouble
And it's just not fair at all.

Although sometimes she can be funny
She's good fun too
We have great fun sometimes
So in the end she's an OK sister.

Craig Devereux (9)
Knoxland Primary School, Dumbarton

HIDDEN TREASURE

Hidden treasure is finding out my long lost gran is coming to stay.
Hidden treasure is because I've not seen her in fifty years.
Hidden treasure is the letter she sent to me.
Hidden treasure is her remembering my birthday.
Hidden treasure is the photo she sent me.
Hidden treasure is the photo that filled a gap in my heart.
Hidden treasure is never letting go of the memories I have.
Hidden treasure is the presents, photos and other things she sends me.
My treasure is knowing she will always fill a gap in my heart.

Kevin Harrison (11)
Knoxland Primary School, Dumbarton

THE UNIVERSE

Jupiter, Saturn, Uranus and Mars,
Are some of the planets
High above the stars.
Pluto is the smallest they say
Also it is further away.
The sun lights up the Earth so bright,
It gives us heat and also light.
It keeps us warm with every ray,
When it comes out to brighten our day.
The moon shines down at night,
It shines so very bright,
It shines like a light
In the dead of night.

David Allen (10)
Knoxland Primary School, Dumbarton

PUSSY CAT

A little fluffy kitty
Likes a woolly ball
He likes to run, jump and have some fun
Sometimes he's scared
Sometimes he's not
He's orangy-yellow
With lovely green eyes
He fits in a fluffy hat
That's my fluffy pussy cat.

Alexander Shreenan (9)
Knoxland Primary School, Dumbarton

THE FOREST

In the forest trees blow from side to side
I see the squirrels hide
I also hear the mole
Who is digging a hole
The rabbit is eating a carrot
That's his habit
It hops everywhere
But as quiet as can be
He creeps out of sight
Into the dark, dark forest.

Emily Kirkwood (9)
Knoxland Primary School, Dumbarton

THE WEIRD PIGEON

I saw a pigeon in the sky
And guess what he was holding? A pie!
I said to myself, I must be dreaming
But then I began to fly
Straight into the pie!
The pigeon said sorry, that he didn't mean it,
But I knew that was a lie.

Emma Ritchie (10)
Knoxland Primary School, Dumbarton

MY NORMAL DAY

When I wake up in the morning
The sun is always dawning
I hear the crows cawing
And mice gnawing

I get dressed
When my room is all messed
I hear the birds in their nests

I creep down the stair
But it isn't fair
I can't brush my hair
Because I can't find my comb anywhere

I creep out the door
I don't like it anymore
Because I hurt myself, sore

I creep fast through the gate
So I won't be late
To play with my mate
I run at a fast rate

I finish my day
By talking to Faye
Nearly finished, the 3rd of May
Now it's time for me to say
Goodbye!

Paula Smith (10)
Knoxland Primary School, Dumbarton

MY SCHOOL TRIP

I wake up in the morning
When the sun is dawning,
I run down the stair
To do up my hair.

I went to the park
So no one will nark,
I heard dogs bark
Till it was dark.

I climbed up a tree
Then someone shouted at me,
'Get down before the teacher sees,'
I climbed down the tree
But she didn't see me.

On the way back home
Luckily I had a comb,
'Cause my hair was sticking up
Like a Millennium Dome.

Kyle Proctor (10)
Knoxland Primary School, Dumbarton

ANIMALS

Dogs and cats
Rats and bats
There're thousands of different animals
Like reptiles, birds and mammals
Some are pets, others live in the wild
There're thousands of different animals
Some laugh, sing and smile.

Amanda Smyth (10)
Knoxland Primary School, Dumbarton

WHAT CHRISTMAS IS LIKE

The ice sparkles like crystals and the rooftops are all white,
Santa Claus is coming, so you'd better be out of sight.
Children will be happy with their presents under the tree,
Christmas paper torn everywhere for everyone to see,
Boys make lots of noise with their new toys,
Like *broom, broom, broom* of the bright red car,
The little girl is happy with her new baby doll,
Which says 'Mama! Mama! Mama!' every time she falls.
The day passes quickly with lots of food to eat,
Everyone shuts their eyes, for a little sleep.
When the party games are over, it's time to go to bed,
Goodbye Santa Claus, see you next year and your reindeer.

David Robert Johnston (11)
Knoxland Primary School, Dumbarton

HALLOWE'EN FUN!

H   allowe'en is the time for fun
A   time when vampires scare your mum!
L   ie in bed, awake and scared
L   ingering alone
O   ne thing you think of is that your room is filled with ghosts, but
W   hen midnight strikes, you think, phew, you're fine
E   verybody joins the fun
E   veryone dresses up, but
N   ow Hallowe'en has gone, no one to scare!

Rachel Wilson (10)
Knoxland Primary School, Dumbarton

What Shall I Have For Lunch?

What shall I have for lunch?
There are loads of things to choose from like:

Sandwiches, pasta, fish and chips,
Pizza, crackers and cheese.
What shall I have for lunch?
Oh, what shall I have for lunch?

What shall I have for lunch?
My favourite thing is pasta.
Oh yeah, that's what my mum made me,
Good old Mum!

Lauren McEwan (9)
Knoxland Primary School, Dumbarton

My Teacher

My teacher echoes when she speaks
It sounds like a wolf coming up the street
Even though she's nice and full of life
She's never someone you would like
When she enters the classroom
It feels as if there's an earthquake
When she gets angry she looks like a man from the moon
Even though people thinks she's so *cool*
I think she's cool too
But I still think she's a man from the moon!

Marilyn McGrandle (8)
Knoxland Primary School, Dumbarton

MY LITTLE SISTER

My little sister
Sometimes she's OK
And sometimes she's not.

My little sister
Sometimes she's fun
And sometimes she's not.

My little sister
Sometimes she's greedy
And sometimes she's not.

My little sister
Sometimes she's bossy
And sometimes she's not.

Craig Winslow (9)
Knoxland Primary School, Dumbarton

HOUSES

Some houses are big, some are small
Some are very low down, some are very tall
I like my house, it's okay
But there are a few more places I'd like to stay
Like Buckingham Palace would be grand
Or a farm would be a mucky land
These are some places I'd like to stay
But my house is good enough for me anyway.

Aimee Trainer (9)
Knoxland Primary School, Dumbarton

IT WASN'T ME

Who left the TV on?
Who wrote on the wall?
Who ran the pen out?
Who left the phone on call?

Who left the fridge open?
Who ate the cheese?
Who drank the wine?
Who forgot the keys?

Who spilt the orange juice?
Who drank the tea?
Who ate the biscuits?
Mum, it wasn't me!

Rosie Smith (10)
Longniddry Primary School, Longniddry

SUNSET

S   un goes down
U   watch the colours change from blue to red to pink
N   ever seen it just like this one
S   un is the beautiful thing of them all
E   veryone loves it
T   op to toe disappears away until the next day.

Joanna Keiller (10)
Longniddry Primary School, Longniddry

HIDDEN TREASURE

Hidden treasure
under the sea,
In a cave
where no one can see.

A boy went under the water
he could see the treasure
under the sea
in the cave.

He went in the cave
and saw the sharks and said,
'This treasure is not for me.'

Dale Gordon (10)
Longniddry Primary School, Longniddry

UNDER THE SEA!

Under the sea there are lots of fish,
and all day long they swish, swosh, swish!
One day the fish found,
a box under the ground.
And inside the box there were
books, tops and a video of the Wizard of Oz.
What were they going to do with it?
I didn't know, but they did!

Farren Brown (11)
Longniddry Primary School, Longniddry

IMAGINE IF . . .

Imagine if . . .
Kids had jobs and adults went to school,
If school dinners were nice enough to make us drool.
If there were houses on the moon,
If we were to eat our crisps - with a spoon!
If teddy bears walked,
If humans squawked.
If we could play all day.
If April Fool's day was in May
And everything was free,
If the world was perfect to some certain degree!

Calvin McDonald (10)
Longniddry Primary School, Longniddry

FIRELIGHT

Here I sit in the dark room, all alone,
With nobody but the fire for company.
The red, orange and purple mix together,
And then tear up the chimney,
Roaring like the Devil himself.

Eventually, I leave the room and go to bed
Leaving the fire to burn out in the night.
But the fire burns on,
The jagged flames dancing their haunting movements.

Sophie Patterson (10)
Longniddry Primary School, Longniddry

FRIENDS FOREVER

B esides what they say
E very day
S ometimes when people are rough
T hree people we stay

F orever we will stay friends
R ebecca is one of my best friends
I ntelligent she is
E normously funny in every way
N ever lets you down
D o you know my other best friend?
S ophie is her name.

Lucy White (10)
Longniddry Primary School, Longniddry

MY RABBIT

My rabbit is called Thumper, he is very sweet,
Carrots, broccoli, sprouts, these are what he eats.
He lives in a metre long hutch,
With loads of hay and sawdust.
Black and white, with a touch of grey,
In his hutch he lies all day.
Dutch is the kind of rabbit he is,
He can lick but he can't kiss.
My rabbit is called Thumper, he is very cute,
He is grey and white and nearly as black as soot.

Lucy Simpson (10)
Longniddry Primary School, Longniddry

TREASURE

Hidden treasure under the sea,
Let's count it, one, two, three.
One silver, one gold,
There's many stories I've been told.
A special cup in a golden chest,
All hunched up with all the rest.
If there's treasure under the sea,
I know who'll get it -

Me, me, me!

David Sked (10)
Longniddry Primary School, Longniddry

LOOK AT ME!

Look at me, I'm flying, see!
I'm in the air,
Come on then, give me a dare.

Look at me, a loop-the-loop,
Give me a bowl of soup.
Look at me, I'm coming in,
Give me my din!

Jamie Greig (10)
Longniddry Primary School, Longniddry

FIRE

Flames dancing here and there,
I like to watch the flames
Bouncing in the air,
Reaching upwards into the sky,
Everlasting, that's fire.

Rebecca Mitchell (10)
Longniddry Primary School, Longniddry

MURKY SEA

In the bottom of the murky sea,
You never know what there might be.
Under stones, in the seaweed,
Fishes swim,
They always win,
In the search for hidden treasure.

Lynsey Smith (9)
Meldrum Primary School, Livingston

HIDDEN TREASURE

Hidden treasure in the deep,
Inside, outside for me to keep,
If I find it, if I don't
I won't be happy, no I won't,
If I find it in a day
I won't have to pay my taxes, yeah!

Robbie Bull (9)
Mid Calder Primary School, Livingston

HIDDEN TREASURES

Hidden treasure in the jungle,
Let's hope the ground doesn't rumble.
It could be in a lake,
Or guarded by a snake.
It could be in a tree,
Or beside the sea.
If I find it, it will be sold,
This will be a tale to be told.

Andrew Iain Summers (9)
Mid Calder Primary School, Livingston

HIDDEN TREASURE

Hidden treasure is in the ground,
If you're lucky it might be found,
Dig for it, if you dare,
But whatever you do, remember to share
Be careful not to get hurt
When you're digging in the dirt.
When you get it, there's one thing to do
Spend it, lend it, just for you!

Phoebe Ridgman (9)
Mid Calder Primary School, Livingston

HIDDEN TREASURES

Down at the bottom of the deep blue sea,
There is something there for you and me
I wonder what it could be?
So come on everybody, let's go and see,
So come with me to the bottom of the deep blue sea.

Mark Cunningham (9)
Mid Calder Primary School, Livingston

HIDDEN TREASURE

H   idden treasure in the dungeon
I   wonder if it is in London?
D   umb or smart, it'll be hard to find,
D   o hope the people in there are kind
E   veryone doesn't know
N   ot to let the secret go,

T   ry your best it will be hard,
R   un to the dungeon, let's hope it isn't barred.
E   veryone will wonder, what's going on?
A   fter all that trouble, it might be gone!
S   o don't built your hopes up,
U   nder there could only be one golden cup.
R   ight deep in the dungeon, there is treasure,
E   very day I'll try to get there in good weather.

Jennifer Logan (9)
Mid Calder Primary School, Livingston

HIDDEN TREASURE

Did you hear about the treasure underneath the sea?
There's golden cups and bits of gold,
I wonder if it's for you and me?
So go down there and look
It could be only one golden book.
It could be high, it could be low, you never know.
It could be hidden, or the place you find it,
Could be strictly forbidden.

Nicola Brash (9)
Mid Calder Primary School, Livingston

HIDDEN TREASURE

Hidden treasure, wonder where it could be?
Maybe my ancestors left it there for me!
Upstairs, downstairs, looking everywhere.

Here! Here! Come and see,
Look what I've found
It's so easy to see.
It's a beautiful box
Let's open it!

Oh, it hasn't got a key!
Here it is.
'Open it!' says a voice - a ghost it must be.

I open it and it's a picture of an ancestor of mine,
It's my great, great gran, drinking some wine.
I'll show my mum and dad.
My mum and dad are very glad!

Joanna Pringle (9)
Mid Calder Primary School, Livingston

HIDDEN TREASURE

Deep, deep down in the dirty ground,
There lies some treasure that must be found.
There's golden rings and lots of things,
Watch out for the traps,
There could be rats.
There will be old gold
I've been told!
I can't wait,
Because I'm going to get it at this *rate!*

Joel McDiarmid (9)
Mid Calder Primary School, Livingston

HIDDEN TREASURE

H idden at the bottom of the deep blue sea
I t is something for you and me
D id you hear?
D id you hear?
E verbody, did you hear?
N ow you know the secret.

T reasure is hidden at the bottom of the deep blue sea
R ise, everybody get moving
E verybody get cruising
A s you can see you were desperate to find the treasure
S end the scuba-diver in
U nless you want to run in
R est just now, because you're going in
E verybody is cheering for him.

Aimee Nelson (9)
Mid Calder Primary School, Livingston

HIDDEN TREASURE

Down at the bottom of the garden,
There is something there, but no one knows where,
There are some treasures, but nobody knows
What it could be?
Look hard and you might find it for me.
If you find it, remember to share,
Don't be greedy, you must take care.

Cheryl Hadden (9)
Mid Calder Primary School, Livingston

HIDDEN TREASURE

Treasure, treasure where could it be?
Treasure, treasure it could be under me
So I will go down to the cellar
To see what I can see.

Down, down in the cellar
Down, down in the sea.
There might be some treasure
Just for me.

There might be some gold
Or some silver for me to hold
But if it is, it must be sold.

Louise Hogg (9)
Mid Calder Primary School, Livingston

HIDDEN TREASURE

Hidden treasure buried in the sand,
If you're lucky, you might find it man!
Diamonds, emeralds, rubies, silver and gold,
If I found it, every bit of it would be sold.
Maybe some to keep
But now I'm searching in the sea that's deep.
Now I'm searching on the land,
Then I find it in the sand.

Michael Robert Mair (8)
Mid Calder Primary School, Livingston

HIDDEN TREASURE

Hidden treasure just for me
Hidden treasure just for me
Where could it be?
Where could it be?
Hidden treasure just for me

It could be here
It could be there
It could be anywhere.

I've found it now!
I've found it now!
I don't know how!
I've found it now!

Rachael King (9)
Mid Calder Primary School, Livingston

HIDDEN TREASURE

It could be hidden in the basement,
It could be hidden at the beach.
But no one knows where it is
Pirates are to find it,
When it's lying under the sea.
Then I find the pot of gold,
That no one has ever found before.

Craig Merritt (9)
Mid Calder Primary School, Livingston

HIDDEN TREASURE

Did you hear about the treasure
Underneath the sea,
In a cave
With all the animals,
What could it be?
Could it be beside an octopus?
Could it be in a whale?
All of them are scary
You will need a fairy.

Thomas Fraser (9)
Mid Calder Primary School, Livingston

HIDDEN TREASURE

Hidden treasure in the sea,
It might be easy, it might not be.
You will need a submarine,
If you're in the Royal Marines.
You might sell it or you might keep it,
It's up to you what you want to do.

Ryan Stuart Gray (9)
Mid Calder Primary School, Livingston

THE DAY I MET MOLLY THE MONSTER

One day when I was walking down the street
I didn't know that I was going to meet
a big monster with twelve eyes,
honest I'm not telling any lies.
I was really scared of it,
then it came to me and said
'Do you have a first-aid kit?'
It had a thorn stuck in its paw
and then a big yawn came out of its jaw.
Her name was Molly Black
and her boss had just given her the sack.
She had been walking for days on end
trying to find her very best friend.
She said she fell in a deep hole
which had just been dug by a mole.
There was the thorn that went in her hand
and she said she'd never forget that land.
We talked for a little while
and then she told me about her best friend Kyle.
I took the thorn and put it in the bin
and then I told her all about my kin.
After a while, she went away
maybe to go and play.
I never ever saw her again
but I think I saw her Uncle Den.

Laura Mair Reid (11)
Milton Primary School, Dumbarton

THE STARS

I gaze upon the sky tonight
I wonder if the stars are bright
I look for hours, so I might see
Just one star to name after me.

I gaze upon the sky tonight
There's lots of clouds, no stars, no light
It's raining now and I can't see
A single star or moon for me.

I gaze upon the sky tonight
I see one, no, it's out of sight
I'm getting bored 'cause I can't see
A single star to name after me.

I gaze upon the sky tonight
Where have they gone?
Who has stolen the light?
I'll keep watch just in case
I see a star that I might chase.

I gaze upon the sky tonight
A million stars I see in flight
I'll make a wish and if it's true
I'll see you tomorrow when the sky's not blue.

Kimberly Gledhill (11)
Milton Primary School, Dumbarton

I'D LIKE TO GO TO SPAIN

I'd like to go to Spain flying
in an aeroplane.

I'd like to go to Spain lying
on the sandy beach.

I'd like to go to Spain spying
on my friends.

I'd like to go to Spain playing
in the arcade again.

I'd like to go to Spain and see
the sun, sand and sea again.

Sun, sand and sea is where
I feel free, sun, sand and sea
is the life for me.

Plane, Spain, Spain, plane
now I'm back home
in the rain again.

Richard Anderson (11)
Milton Primary School, Dumbarton

I SAW A ...

I saw a lion sitting on the bed,
I saw a lion dancing on its head,
I saw a lion putting on a hat,
I saw a lion making itself fat.

I saw a tiger chewing up a shoe,
I saw a tiger sitting in the zoo,
I saw a tiger standing up straight,
I saw a tiger talking to its mate.

I saw a panda cuddling up tight,
I saw a panda having a fight,
I saw a panda looking at the stars,
I saw a panda eating some Mars bars.

I saw a monkey looking round and round,
I saw a monkey bouncing up and down,
I saw a monkey telling a story (it's true)
I saw a monkey and it looked just like you!

Lara Stockley (11)
Milton Primary School, Dumbarton

I SAW A TIGER IN THE JUNGLE

I saw a tiger in the jungle,
He had black stripes.
He was a good listener,
He had sharp teeth and good eyesight.
He had orange skin, sharp claws,
Long tail.
He hides now in the jungle,
He runs dead fast, chasing other animals.
He moves quietly to get his dinner
So beware!
Mornings - he's at the pond
For a drink and hunts for his breakfast.
He has a big roar in the morning,
Sometimes they come in groups of two
To quickly catch animals.
He lives in the wild, ready to pounce
On animals.

James Mitchell (11)
Milton Primary School, Dumbarton

MY DREAM

My dream is to be an astronaut
and fly to the moon
My dream is to see all the
planets and their moons
My dream is to be a monster
and scare kids at night
My dream is to be Harry Potter
and learn magic
My dream is to be a bug
and scare people
My dream is to be a stuntman
and do dangerous stunts

And I really want to help the world.

Graham Kirkwood
Milton Primary School, Dumbarton

HOLIDAYS

When we get school holidays,
I would like some fun
in the sun.
When I go somewhere sunny,
I would probably like it more.

When I get holidays in the sun,
I want to go to Orlando,
To have fun in the sun.

When I'm older I will go with my friends
To somewhere cold for a change,
But soon there will be no more fun in the sun.

James Lacey (11)
Milton Primary School, Dumbarton

MY CAT LANCELOT

My cat Lancelot, he really likes to prance a lot
He's really a big softy, but thinks he's hard as toffee
My cat Lancelot, he likes to dance a lot
We bought him in a shop
He did a big hop
He jumps on walls
And likes sitting in halls
We stroke him every day
And then he runs away
He likes to chase rats
And fights with other cats
When he's in a mood
He doesn't like food
He likes following me
But doesn't like tea.

Chris Cunningham (10)
Milton Primary School, Dumbarton

MY DOG CALLED HEATHER

My dog called Heather
She's the type of dog, a real blather.
She moans all the time, looking for cheese
And never says please.
She is a dog, good even in the rain
Oh such a lovely collie
Me with my hood and her with her brolly.

Scott Mitchell (11)
Milton Primary School, Dumbarton

IF I WAS A WIZARD

If I was a wizard
I'd conjure up things to my liking
Maybe a bike to go biking

If I was a wizard
I'd go into the future
To see my friend as a butcher

If I was a wizard
I'd conjure up things galore
I'd play and play and play until it became a bore

If I was a wizard
I'd fly away to Mars
Just to see their cool hovercars

If I was a wizard
I'd conjure up money, money, money
And make myself really, really, funny

If I was a wizard
I wouldn't go to school
I'd made myself very smart and act really cool

If I wizard
I'd laugh and shout with glee
But sadly enough I'm just me

Shaun Duff Bruce (10)
Milton Primary School, Dumbarton

DOLPHINS

D olphins are my fave
  they love to laugh and play,
O ceans and the seas are their loving homes
  of all the types of dolphins, the bottlenose is my love.
L ovely, cute and cuddly I can mould
  a dolphin out of clay.
P retty, nice and blue, they
  make me happy when skies are grey.
H ere with me today, I have two cuddly toys
  dolphins called *Danny* and *Dave,*
I 'm going to be swimming
  with them in September.
N ot only are they what I've said
  they're also very tender.

Louise Rae (11)
Milton Primary School, Dumbarton

TELEVISION

Oh great, I'm home from school
Tired, I feel like I could sleep for a week.
I shuffle through to the living room
All I want to do is flop down on the couch
And watch CBBC.
But wait! What's this? Winter athletics!
I can't believe it!
How boring.
I can't believe anyone would watch it.
I know, I'll write a complaint.
Maybe this one will be sent
Along with the other five I wrote earlier this week.

Jo Stewart (11)
Muirhead Primary School, Troon

COLOURS

I see a red-hot sizzling fire
Burning in the night.
I see a boiling hot sun
Shining in the light.
I see strawberries
Waiting to be picked.

I see the clear sky
With not a cloud in sight.
I see blue cold ice
Which looks very slippery.
I see dark sky
With a bright moon in it.

I see a bright yellow sun
But not as hot as red.
I see people
Wearing yellow T-shirts.
I see teenagers
Wearing yellow vest tops.

Sarah Berry (11)
Muirhead Primary School, Troon

SIGHT

Red is like a juicy strawberry,
Just waiting to be picked,
Taking your first bite is mouth-watering,
With the juice running everywhere.

Blue is like the sky on a warm summer's day,
In winter, blue is a cold colour,
But best of all it is calm,
Calm as can be.

Gold is like a summer's day sun,
Shining down on us,
Keeping us warm,
Which is really nice.

Gayle Douglas (11)
Muirhead Primary School, Troon

CONVERSATION PIECE

'Thompson where is your homework?'
'Here it is Sir,'
'What is this?'
'What does it look like?'
'What on earth happened to it?'
'I found it in the dustbin Sir.'
'A dustbin! That explains everything.'
'Why Sir?'
'I want you to rewrite this at break.'
'Okay.'
'You didn't address me as Sir.'
'I know.'
'Do this ten times and you have an appointment with the belt.'
'That'll be fine.'
'Now twenty times over and twenty minutes of the belt.'
'That's a shame.'

Graeme Currie (11)
Muirhead Primary School, Troon

KAYLEIGH

My dog named Kayleigh, has golden brown hair,
She's scared of the wind when it roars,
If she hears a noise outside she hides under my covers.
When I sit alone, she will come up to me
And cuddle into me.
When my mum comes to put me to bed,
She will come too.
She tries to protect me all the time.
When I take her for a walk, she is very pleased,
With a big wag of her tail, we feel happy together.
Her very soft hair gets up my nose,
I sneeze, she runs away.
She sleeps in my mum's room,
She is scared of cats and never hurts a soul.
That's my dog, Kayleigh.

Mhairi Hynd (11)
Muirhead Primary School, Troon

THE VIOLENT STORM

The wind was violent.
It was breaking the tiles off the roof
And crashing against the window.
The wind was making loud bangs,
People were getting blown away.
Birds flying from side to side.
The wind was like a big bird landing,
The wind was like a roaring plane,
The wind was very strong,
The wind was snapping branches,
The doors rattled and banged.

Kayleigh Davies (8)
Muirhead Primary School, Troon

MY FRIEND

My friend helps me when I am sad
he always makes me glad.
I throw him a ball
down the hall
he always brings it back to me
oh what a lovely friend is he.
I take him to the beach
then take him back home
then he will always moan.
If he doesn't get his dinner
he will get thinner and thinner.
He is my best friend.

Blain Seffen (10)
Muirhead Primary School, Troon

THE STORM

Tiles crashing, smashing off the wall
The wind howling

Creaking roofs
Cars, vans blown over
Cottage windows creaking and rattling at the door

In fields cows running under shelters
Trees snapping and lying on grass

Slabs bursting off the ground and flying onto the road
Greenhouses smashing.

Siobhan Carr (8)
Muirhead Primary School, Troon

EASTER EGGS

Easter eggs are yummy
They fill my tummy
Big ones and little ones
I have tons

The Easter bunny comes along
Sometimes he sings an Easter song
He hides the eggs around the house

I have to search high and low
For the eggs that we all love so
I find them here I find them there
I even find them under the stair

Then all that's left for me to do
Is eat them all before you do!

Iain Finnie (9)
Muirhead Primary School, Troon

MY BEST FRIEND

My best friend is Tracey
When she's funny
It's always very sunny
She always makes me laugh
When we are in the cafe
She makes me laugh so much
I fall on the ground
And then I spin around
And I drop my pound.

Lindsay Haswell (8)
Muirhead Primary School, Troon

MY COUSIN

My cousin has long, golden hair
She has a big brother who is usually unfair
My cousin has a little brother who is very, very cute
Her brother Liam can be a brute.

She has a hamster who can do the monkey bars
She also likes chocolate bars
My cousin Erin is quite tall
Her little brother Ryan is very small.

I think my cousin is the best
I think she is better than all the rest
My cousin's heart is not cold
For my cousin has a heart of gold.

Katie Gilgallon (9)
Muirhead Primary School, Troon

UNTITLED

I play rugby, oh yes I do
If you play I'll tackle you
When it rains it is very muddy
When I fall I look very funny
The coach is good at teaching us
When I feel tired I get home by bus.

Sean Mitchell (10)
Muirhead Primary School, Troon

THE STORM ATTACK

The tiles crashed from the creaking roofs
The houses rattled side to side
The wind howled loudly

The crashing, splashing waves collided with the wall
The fierce wind got stronger
The debris flew across the beach

The trees uprooted
The branches broke off the trees and crashed to the ground.

Megan Humphreys (9)
Muirhead Primary School, Troon

THE WIND

The wind is like a lion roaring in the night
The wind gave me a fright
The wind is like a giant banging on the door
Rattling the windows and shaking the floor
The wind is like an army shooting at the house
The wind is like a wolf howling in the night.

Shauna Berry (8)
Muirhead Primary School, Troon

WHEN I GROW UP

When I grow up
I'm going to be a policeman
I want to be a fireman
I don't know what I will be.

I will be a Rangers football player
I will be a mechanic
What should I be?

I want to be a lot of things
I wish I could do them all!

Kieran Cook (9)
Muirhead Primary School, Troon

MY DOG, SWEEP

We have a dog called Sweep
so curly and so sweet
and every time we have some sweets
he barks and tries to bite our feet.

Christina Fulton (10)
Muirhead Primary School, Troon

HIDDEN TREASURE

Gold, silver and diamonds,
Everyone has these,
A special hidden treasure.
But where, where do they hide it?
Is there a place.

Where do you keep your gold?
Do you know of it because there is no 'X' to mark the spot,
Where do your friends and family keep their treasure?
Do they know? Do they even know?
Ask them and find out.

The happiest person in the world has no gold,
He has no secret treasure,
Does he need any?
But yet poor men
Have all the gold they need.

I know where my treasure is,
It's inside me, in my soul.
But no! I haven't eaten gold or jewels,
I have a secret wish, like everyone else,
Which are my diamonds.

Go hunting for your treasure,
But don't bother buying tickets to desert islands!
You're not Captain Hook or Peter Pan,
You're like me, a normal person
And I hope you find all your treasure!

Has anyone found their treasure yet?
Their deepest desire, their fortune?
Remember, not everyone finds their silver,
They're not lucky, they can't gold,
But I hope all of you are among the most fortunate.

Brendan Musk (11)
Parkhead Primary School, West Calder

HIDDEN TREASURE

Use your imagination, let it run wild.
Think you are in a different world,
there is a shovel in your hand,
underneath your feet is sand.
You dig and dig and dig.

And it feels like you've found a treasure chest
full of jewels and gold.
Because in this little world you're in,
you've done exactly as I just told.

You get ever so excited, so that in a flash,
a hurried dash, your treasure's gone,
it's spent and it won't come back.

If you come back to our world,
you'll find that your energy has gone.
That was the treasure inside the chest,
your energy is gold, your imagination is the jewel you sold.
Did you notice they were spic and span and covered in no mould!

The little world was your heart,
you never left this world at all.
But I hope I've taught you:

You need not look for treasure,
for it is already deep inside you.

Kirsty MacDonald (10)
Parkhead Primary School, West Calder

HIDDEN TREASURE

I have a secret
I'll bet so do you,
But when you hear mine
It will make you feel fine
It is about my great hidden treasure
And it gives me lots of pleasure.

I'll give you a clue
It's not very new.

You may see it every day
But what can I say
Goodbye, good luck
Then again maybe not
But before you reach the end I'll tell you.
That my hidden treasure
Is my best friend!

Amy Thomson (11)
Parkhead Primary School, West Calder

TREASURE ISLAND

Is it hidden underwater?
Is it hidden underground?
Is it hidden in the bushes?
Is it waiting to be found?

Is it in a dark and gloomy place
Or is it somewhere in the sun?
Is it lots of shining treasure
Or is it just enough for one?

Will we ever find it?
Is it really true
Or is it just something to dream about . . .
A dream for me and you?

Rachel McConnell (10)
Parkhead Primary School, West Calder

A WINTER DREAM!

Outside my window,
I see snow
And children's faces
Light up and glow.

Listen to the sound of
The robin singing,
Mixed with the sound
Of sleigh bells
Ringing.

The trees are cold,
Frosty and bare,
Oh how it must seem so
Chilly out there.

Now it's night,
There's sparkle in the air
And all I seem to do is glare.

When it's time for bed
And we are all cosy,
The fire's burning and
Our cheeks go rosy.

Stacey Whyte (11)
Parkhead Primary School, West Calder

HIDDEN TREASURE

On an island far away,
Looking for the treasure,
With the map in my hand,
I'm looking left and right.

Where do I go? What do I do?
Where do I find this treasure?
I scan the fine print on the map,
Then I stare at the ground - and measure.

Turning to the left,
I march towards the trees,
Looking back and forth,
Let me find the right way,
Oh please!

I've found a great big cross!
It looks like I am rich,
I dig, dig, dig, below,
Below the surface of the ground.

Something hard,
A box!
I haul it out,
Snap open the lid with all my force,
And, and, and . . .

It's empty!

Fiona Rennie (10)
Parkhead Primary School, West Calder

HARRY POTTER POEM

Thy tiny little Snitch,
Flies wondrously on thy pitch,
Thy fast, ugly Bludger
Al yi dae is git smugger,
Oh yi blood-red Quaffle
Al yi dae is make this affale.

In school there's alwiz a quiet motion
When yer making' a thick ugly potion,
At the amazin' tasty lunch
Everyone wants a great munch,
A good, cheerful charm
Doesn't do any harm.

So never cast a spell on a friend
Or you'll have ti dae the mend
And that old Quidditch teacher, Madam Hooch
Plays a lot wi her tinsy white pooch
There's alwiz tiny Professor Flitwick
He has a charmy old trick.

Sly old Professor Snape
Hid behind a big, purple drape.
Big, grumpy three-headed Fluffy
Al yi wanna dae is be ruffy.
Ind when yer on the Hogwarts train
On the way there's alwiz a bit eh rain.

Jamie Bowman (10)
Parkhead Primary School, West Calder

WHERE CAN THE TREASURE BE?

I really can't think where the treasure can be
It could be on land or in the sea.
I've looked high and low and everywhere you go
But where it is I do not know.

I asked my friend to help me look
But all she did was play her flute.
The magic then made me think of the sea
And I then was sure that's where it would be.

The next day I went under the sea
And to my surprise there it was staring at me.

Lori Davidson (10)
Parkhead Primary School, West Calder

PETER

Peter would be perfect if he was never sad,
Peter would be cool if he did not get treated bad,
Peter would be happy if he didn't wear dirty clothes,
Peter would be clean if he scrubbed his toes,
Peter likes to wander around all alone,
Peter always shouts in class in a high tone,
Peter only combs his hair with an old comb,
But Peter says to everyone,
'At least I have a home.'

Kimberley Crossan (10)
Rosewell Primary School, Rosewell

MY GRAN

My gran was kind,
Her heart was stuck together with glue,
Made of love.
But now the bomb has dropped with
Cancer gas.
Death has reached my gran's soul.
I miss her laugh,
I miss her smile,
At night with water in my eyes
A bright star I see, to be my gran,
When I hear about Gran,
I think about her young heart.

Conner McConnell (8)
Rosewell Primary School, Rosewell

TALIBAN

Why did the Talibans do such a thing?
First the Twin Towers, now trying to win
Taliban put sorrow in American's eyes,
Taliban demolished American's pride.
Terrible destruction by Taliban,
Why did they do this?
Why did they destroy a citizen's dream?
Why did they kill such innocent people?
Taliban scarified America's beauty,
Taliban are such an evil gang,
Destroyed beauty in American's life.

David Kyle (10)
Rosewell Primary School, Rosewell

SEPTEMBER THE 11TH

On September the 11th,
Panic started to spread
From the plane flying,
The people were dying,
On September the 11th.

When the hijacked plane
Got flown into the Twin Towers,
People were shocked,
After the incident on September the 11th.

The sky was grey, coming from the Twin Towers,
After the planes crashing powers,
Almost 3,000 people killed,
On September the 11th.

Grief was caused by the Taliban,
Police cars and fire engines were all
There trying to clear the rubble,
But it was no use,
The Taliban had demolished America's pride,
On September the 11th.

Andrew McLay (9)
Rosewell Primary School, Rosewell

WHY?

Why, why does it happen?
Who really wants to kill?
Who sacrifices thousands of lives,
Not just their own,
Lives, they don't control?

Why does it happen?
Please tell me why?
Devastation in people's eyes,
Tell me why they kill?

Louise Arnott (10)
Rosewell Primary School, Rosewell

RAINFOREST MONKEY

I am a monkey who lives in a forest,
A rainforest to be exact,
My friend is a chimp
And we like to limp,
But the forest is beginning to die.

Man is destroying the rainforest,
Our rainforest to be exact,
Our old climbing tree,
Has happened to be,
Knocked down by the cutting machine.

I ask you to stop your destruction,
Your destruction to be exact,
If you do not stop,
We'll be left to hop,
Through the destructive mess.

Rona Anderson (11)
Rosewell Primary School, Rosewell

COME AND SEE ROSEWELL

Rosewell has many big hills,
It's beautiful to see,
There are lots of trees too,
Where people walk their dogs,
Just like me.

To live in Rosewell is very funky,
My friends and I act like monkeys,
We jump around in circles
And swing from tree to tree,
It's fun for my friends
And fun for me.

The fields are great when they're mucky
And I don't even mind getting dirty,
When I look all around at the best view,
I feel happy and lucky,
To live in Rosewell.

Jamie Goodall (11)
Rosewell Primary School, Rosewell

DESTRUCTION

Afghanistan, America, battling to the ground,
India, volcanoes, getting too hot, earthquakes,
People dying, pain, people crying again and again.

Volcanoes erupting and exploding sounds,
Dead bodies always being found,
Babies are dying and parents are crying,
Rivers of lava flowing down the streets,
Dead people,
God always meets.

Sean Crossan (9)
Rosewell Primary School, Rosewell

To Live In Rosewell

To live in Rosewell
And the school's loud bell.

The colourful park,
Lots of dogs bark.

Mums' buying,
Children crying.

Vandals on the street,
Lots of people to meet.

To live in Rosewell,
Everyone's well.

Nichole McGregor (10)
Rosewell Primary School, Rosewell

I Wish...

I wish I had a sports car,
I wish I could meet a footballer,
I wish I had a motorbike,
I wish to donate a million pounds to charity,
I wish David Beckham was my dad,
I wish Michael Owen was my brother's uncle,
I wish I could go to a rugby match,
I wish I could go to Livingston Skatepark,
I wish Bin Laden would stop the war.

Callum Kyle (8)
Rosewell Primary School, Rosewell

WAR!

Our fellow humans die, the destruction!
Come to our side if you dare.

Our homes reduced to rubble,
What have those men done?
We cry for freedom,
Death has come and taken our brothers' souls.

White and black at war,
Seas fill up with blood!
Souls shall go up but we'll never give up.

The black will take on the white,
The two sides will die in the fight,
The destruction can't be undone,
We will never give up for freedom.

Craig McGregor (11)
Rosewell Primary School, Rosewell

EARTHQUAKE

Earthquakes are very destructive,
They are strong and terrible,
People running and screaming,
Everywhere around the streets,
Churches and hotels are all destroyed,
Rocks and metal falling down,
People getting hurt badly,
Close to death.

Mark Sinanovic (9)
Rosewell Primary School, Rosewell

WORLD WAR TWO

W ar begins,
O nly men are sent to fight,
R adar alarms blare in the distance,
L adies wave farewell to troops,
D estruction of Pearl Harbour.

W ar declared by Britain and France,
A ll plans have been destroyed,
R eloading of troops' drone guns.

T roops get promoted,
W ar ends,
O ne name will stand above all.

Darren Skilbeck (9)
Rosewell Primary School, Rosewell

I WISH

I wish people were really magic,
I wish I could be in two places at once,
I wish you could make someone be your brother in a flash,
I wish monsters really existed,
I wish my sister would stop picking on me,
I wish I had a brother,
I wish the rainforests weren't being destroyed,
I wish all my dreams would come true,
I wish the best for you.

Stewart Roy (9)
Rosewell Primary School, Rosewell

TORNADOES

Tornadoes are destructive,
Their winds are very strong,
Lifting heavy objects,
People flee in terror, running from their homes,
Cars and buses fly, families run to seek shelter,
People in homes and bunkers hope they will
Live through the awful storm,
When the storm is over,
Families are left broken-hearted.

Euan Hamilton (8)
Rosewell Primary School, Rosewell

SEPTEMBER THE ELEVENTH

September the 11th was devastating,
People have lost their lives and families,
Children are scared and worried,
Wondering what will happen next?
Pieces of buildings flying everywhere,
Cars being crushed,
People hanging out of buildings,
Waiting for their lives to be over.

April Clark (10)
Rosewell Primary School, Rosewell

IF ONLY

If only I was born in Africa,
If only I could sail to sea,
If only I was a soldier
Flying over Scottish seas,
If only I could disguise myself as a woman,
If only I could see a football player,
If only I could be myself,
If only, if only.

Katie Neil (9)
Rosewell Primary School, Rosewell

BED

Beds are the greatest couch in the whole world,
My bed makes me feel like I'm in the hottest
Place in the whole world.
My bed makes me feel like I'm the greatest
Person in the whole world.
I love the warmness of my bed.
I wish I could stay in bed all day long.
My mum won't let me stay,
She says, 'Get out of bed and go to school!'
My bed is really bouncy,
I love my bed.

Mairi MacInnes (9)
St Columba's RC Primary School, Oban

MY HAMSTER

My hamster is white like snow,
It is like a little fat furball,
It is like a soft sofa,
It is like the sun on a sunny day,
My hamster is like a wild tiger
When he is annoyed.

Damian McAuley (9)
St Columba's RC Primary School, Oban

MY GUINEA PIG

My guinea pig is black as night,
He is like my soft pillow,
He loves summer because I take him out the back,
He loves apples and carrots,
He likes sunny days when I play with him all day long.

Sophie McCartney (8)
St Columba's RC Primary School, Oban

MY WORST NIGHTMARE

My worst nightmare is as black as a bat,
It's like a dinosaur chasing me,
It is like the night when the moon just rises,
It's like a really stormy day with
Lightning striking a tree.

David Murphy (8)
St Columba's RC Primary School, Oban

MY MUM

My mum is like summer because she is warm when I hug her,
She's like a teddy bear that I hug when I get scared,
My mum is like the morning when the sun rises,
She is like an apple because her cheeks are rosy-red when she smiles,
She is like a lamb because she is beautiful and gentle.

Rona Anderson (8)
St Columba's RC Primary School, Oban

FRIENDS

Friends are fun,
Friends are good but sometimes make me in a bad mood,
But most of the time they make me feel happy,
Everyone in the world should have a friend.

Sean Cooke (8)
St Columba's RC Primary School, Oban

MY MUM

My mum is the colour of the sun on a hot sunny day,
My mum is a nice, big, cuddly sofa,
My mum is like a rainbow in the sky,
My mum is like a bird that can fly very high.

Katherine Jackson (8)
St Columba's RC Primary School, Oban

My Pet Cat

My pet cat is as black as night,
He is like a monster in disguise,
If my cat was a piece of furniture
He would be a sofa because he is so lazy,
My cat Inky is like a storm with thunder
And lightning and rain,
He is like a mini black panther
That sleeps in the middle of the jungle,
Even though my cat is very vicious and tough,
He mostly just wants to play.

Cara Potts (9)
St Columba's RC Primary School, Oban

My Worst Nightmare

My worst nightmare is as green as the grass,
It's like a big, big shark flying around me,
It comes when I go to sleep to sow bad dreams into me,
I feel terrified in my nightmares and try to get away,
The nightmare is as scary as Dracula,
I wish he would haunt someone else
But I always wake up before my death,
To find it's eight o'clock.

Vernon Davies (9)
St Columba's RC Primary School, Oban

FRIENDS

Friends make me feel happy,
Friends are kind,
Friends are considerate,
Friends are respectful,
Friends forgive each other,
Friends are caring too,
Friends help each other
Whatever happens to you.

Zoe Watkins (8)
St Columba's RC Primary School, Oban

FOOTBALL POEM

Football, football,
It's so good,
I can play when I'm in any kind of mood.

Sunshine, rain to me,
It's all the same,
Sometimes I win,
Sometimes I lose
But who cares, I'm a cool dude,
My friends come round and
We start to play football,
Football for the whole day,
David, Declan, Calvin, Ryan and Jason
Are all in my team,
It's a different day,
But we'll all play football today,
Pals United are here to stay.

Lloyd Swann (9)
St Gabriel's Primary School, Prestonpans

AT SCHOOL

School is a fun place to be,
Lots to do and lots to see,
I can play with all my mates, but
Never dare to go out the gates.

First of all we sit and pray,
And prepare the work for the day,
I enjoy reading, it's such fun,
I like to read to everyone.

I like maths as well because I
Like to work things out for myself,
It's not too hard and not too easy,
Just a little easy peasy.

When the lunch bell rings, we all
Think of nice things,
We go to the dinner hall to get some food,
It tastes yummy and good.

After lunch we go to play,
We have lots of things to do and say,
Run 'n' trout and football running fast,
Making sure that we don't fall.

I have fun with all my friends,
And see them sometimes when school ends,
Jennifer, Lauren, Rosalind and Taelor to name but some,
Actually I'm friends with everyone,
At 3.15pm it's time to go home,
I walk with my friends and never alone,
I always try to be good and never be rude.

Amanda Neil McLean (10)
St Gabriel's Primary School, Prestonpans

MY TALENT

School . . . friends what are the best,
Let's put you to the test,
Then this will get rid of all pests,
Because I am the best at what I do.
Let me finish and I'll come and play with you.
I've got the ball at my feet,
A dribble here, a dribble there,
I'll kick the ball into the air,
I've scored a goal, I'll celebrate,
Now the score is 13-8,
We are the champions, we won the cup,
If anyone's better please stand up.

Sam Killen (9)
St Gabriel's Primary School, Prestonpans

MY MUM

My mum worries about me
Getting hurt or if I fall off my skateboard.
She brings me juice and crisps and
Let's me watch TV in my room if I'm good.

When I get up late for school,
She helps me get to school in time for the bell.
My mum cares for me when I'm sick,
She makes me feel better.

My mum's name is Elaine,
No other mum is better than my mum.

Stewart Anderson (9)
St Gabriel's Primary School, Prestonpans

Night Of The Storm

The night was dark and stormy,
Two boys were out alone,
Ghosts and ghouls and creatures,
Chill them to the bone.

Arriving at a cottage,
They walked into the dark, creepy house,
Then they shouted,
'Is anyone home?'
The rain continued to pour.

They walked into the dark, creepy house
And wandered into the living room,
It was so quiet, they could hear a mouse,
Then there was a thunderbolt,
Boom!

It went quiet again,
The boys were very scared,
Then they heard footsteps,
Overhead, upstairs!

As they ran away they fell
And landed in a pile,
Then they heard someone call,
'It's me,' said granny with a smile.

Leah Scott (9)
St Gabriel's Primary School, Prestonpans

My Space Poem

Sing a song of spaceships,
Flying very high,
Four and twenty monkeys,
Flying in the sky.

When the monkeys were gone,
An alien came to me,
It said that I was stupid,
And stuck its tongue out at me.

Ryan Liam McKendrick (8)
St Gabriel's Primary School, Prestonpans

MOON ROCK

C omets land
O n
N eptune
S ick
T ravellers
E at
L ots of
L ovely moon rock
A t
T he
I ntergalactic spacestation
O h
N utritious
S tuff!

A re you
R eady to
E at moon rock?

F abulous moon rock,
A fter a comet came and
B rought it to Neptune.

Megan Lappin (8)
St Gabriel's Primary School, Prestonpans

ME

I am nice, I like to eat rice,
I don't like mice, they're not nice.

I am cool, I love school,
The teachers rule, at my school.

I am neat, I eat meat,
When at school, I sit in my seat.

I am fun, I like to run,
Especially in the sun, I am fun.

I am me,
Me
Do you like what you see?

Shannon Garrity
St Gabriel's Primary School, Prestonpans

MY LITTLE SISTER

I fell in love one day last year,
With a girl I hold so very dear,
She is totally gorgeous you'll agree,
I wish that she could marry me.
Her hair is blonde, her eyes are blue,
I know you'll think she's pretty too.
Her legs are short, her fingers long,
To me she could do no wrong,
People ask if we'll be
Misses and mister and I say
No she's my baby sister.

David Glynn (10)
St Gabriel's Primary School, Prestonpans

MY HOME

When I was born
My home was a flat,
I had a room of my own
And a big garden at the back.

When I was five I moved to a house,
In the hut out the back,
There lived a field mouse.

Now I am nine and still in my house,
I have my own room in the attic,
I lie in my bed and think of that mouse,
I wonder where his bed is?

Daniel Clelland (9)
St Gabriel's Primary School, Prestonpans

POEMS

Do all poems have to rhyme?
Do all the words have to be on time?
Will they go fast,
Will they go slow,
To tell the truth I don't know?
Should they be long?
Should they be small?
Should poems be written at all?
I think poems are hard to write,
This one took me all night.

Liam Ough
St Gabriel's Primary School, Prestonpans

THE GALAXY

I love to watch the stars at night
They glow and twinkle and shine so bright
Some are big and some are small
I wish I could reach up and touch them all.

I watch from my window, the moon at night,
It shines on the Earth like a bright, bright light,
Oh how I wish I could touch that light,
Maybe one day I may.

I like to watch the shooting stars,
Especially when they pass by Mars,
Like a rainbow of light so high in the sky,
I love it when they go shooting by.

The moon is such a wonderful sight,
It makes the Earth light up at night,
If only the world was as bright by day,
I'm sure all our troubles would fade away.

Emma Smith (10)
St Gabriel's Primary School, Prestonpans

JANUARY POEM

January, January, January's here,
January is the best time of year.
January is very cold,
I have to wear my thick coat
Which is very old,
On the 20th of January there was a full moon,
It will be February soon,
In February it will be my birthday,
I will be 9 on the 20th day.

Louise Coyle (8)
St Gabriel's Primary School, Prestonpans

THE WIND

The wind is so fast. I like how it makes me fly.
Up here, down there and everywhere.
I have so much fun playing in the wind up in the sky,
It is so much fun.
It blows all the leaves off the trees and
Makes a good breeze,
Oh how I like the wind and the trees in the night, so cold.
Not the ice, it's not so nice,
The wind is so nice, so nice.
In the day the wind is so cold,
It blows my gate and my hedge.
I had my kite up in the sky so high,
It took it away, away in space.

Lauren Paylor (9)
St Gabriel's Primary School, Prestonpans

COLOURS

I like the colours when the fireworks go *boom,*
I like the colours that are in my room.

I like colours nice and bright,
I like colours yellow and white.

I like colours orange and red,
I like the colours that I stare at in my bed.

I like colours lilac and blue,
I like all the colours of the rainbow too.

I like colours black and green,
I like all the colours, if you know what I mean.

Rosalind McAndrew (9)
St Gabriel's Primary School, Prestonpans

SING A SONG OF PLANETS

Sing a song of planets,
Going in a line,
Four and twenty spacemen,
Looking at a pine,
Sing a song of aliens,
Growing very scary,
Four and twenty craters,
Growing interplanetary,
Sing a song of rockets,
Going by in space,
Four and twenty black holes,
Going in a race.
Sing a song of astronauts,
Going by my face,
Four and twenty aliens,
Going at a pace.

Katie McBrierty (8)
St Gabriel's Primary School, Prestonpans

SPACE SIMILES

Space is like a big dump,
It is dark as oil,
It is as silent as a mouse creeping,
It is as mysterious as a wizard,
It is as wide as the sea,
It is as cold as snow,
It is as hard as rocks coming down from the sky,
It is airless,
It is like entertainment.

Kieran Fraser (8)
St Gabriel's Primary School, Prestonpans

I WAS DREAMING

I was dreaming of an adventure,
I could picture in my mind.
I was counting the footsteps to the treasure,
I was about to find.
I had to cross a burn,
Who's banks were about to burst,
But once past the water,
I could put the gold coins in my purse.
Then suddenly I was awake
With alarm, so loud it hurt
And my mum's voice saying
'Ross it's time to go to church.'

Ross Dryburgh (9)
St Gabriel's Primary School, Prestonpans

A WILD NIGHT

It was a wild wintry night,
The trees swayed and the
Leaves blew out of sight.

The rain poured and the rivers flowed,
While the wind roared.

On the sea the seagulls called,
The boats tossed and the sea bossed.

The wind was roaring and howling,
It crashed and bashed,
The damage it did cost us a lot of cash.

Karina Doran (9)
St Gabriel's Primary School, Prestonpans

A POEM IN SPACE

Sing a song of spaceships,
Flying past the sky,
Four and twenty rockets,
Zooming past my eye.

Sing of song of shooting stars,
Shooting way up high,
Four and twenty moons,
Bombing by.

Sing a song of spacemen,
Floating very high,
Four and twenty planets,
Are floating by.

Sing a song of falling stars,
Falling on the ground,
Four and twenty bright stars,
Dropping on the ground.

Ashley Buchanan (9)
St Gabriel's Primary School, Prestonpans

SPACE

Space is like a never-ending world,
It is as dark as black paint,
It is as silent as a mouse,
It is as mysterious as a dinosaur.

Space is as cold as a freezer,
It is as hot as the sun,
It is as dark as night,
It is as vast as the ocean.

Thomas Connachan (8)
St Gabriel's Primary School, Prestonpans

GROOVY ALIENS

A big ugly alien singing on the moon,
L ittle, little planets the size of a spoon,
I ncredible things happen when you're in space,
E ven ugly aliens like the race,
N ear the planets astronauts are floating,
S o big creatures are creaking and croaking.

R ound and round the rockets go,
A million planets, watch them glow,
C lever, clever aliens playing in the snow,
I ncredible things happen, do you know?
N ever, never go up into space,
G oodness knows you could be in the race!

Andrew O'Brien (8)
St Gabriel's Primary School, Prestonpans

POET IN SPACE

Space is like a wide open world,
It is as dark as the skies at night,
It is as silent as a baby sleeping,
It is as mysterious as a temple of doom.

Space is a very dark place,
It is as cold as Pluto,
It is as hot as the sun.

Space is like a huge big town,
It is bigger than Earth,
It is even bigger than Jupiter.

Emma Yorkston (8)
St Gabriel's Primary School, Prestonpans

THE ALIENS

Sing a song of UFOs,
Up very high,
Four and twenty aliens,
Looking very shy.

Sing a song of astronauts,
Flying through the sky,
Four and twenty aliens,
Eating lots of pies.

Sing a song of rockets,
Zooming in space,
Four and twenty aliens,
Thought it was a race.

Nicky Scott (8)
St Gabriel's Primary School, Prestonpans

MY SPACE POEM

Sing a song of spaceships,
Flying in the sky,
Four and twenty astronauts,
Flying nearby.

Sing a song of planets,
Floating very high,
Four and twenty aliens,
Jumping in the sky.

Paul Glynn (8)
St Gabriel's Primary School, Prestonpans

SPACE POEMS

Sing a song of rockets,
Gliding through the sky,
Four and twenty comets,
Zooming very high.

Sing a song of aliens,
Coming from the moon,
Four and twenty stars,
Going round so soon.

Maria Frazer (8)
St Gabriel's Primary School, Prestonpans

SPACE POEM

Sing a song of spaceships,
Flying through the sky,
Four and twenty planets,
Mostly low then high.

Sing a song of spacemen,
Floating very high, high, high, high.
Four and twenty comets,
Right beside my eye.

Liam White (8)
St Gabriel's Primary School, Prestonpans

MY SPACE POEM

Sing a song of spaceships,
Gliding through the sky,
Four and twenty aliens,
Who look very shy.

Sing a song of comets,
Bashing through the sky,
Four and twenty planets,
Which are very high.

Michael Campbell (8)
St Gabriel's Primary School, Prestonpans

MY SPACE POEM

Space is like a blackboard,
It is dark as black paint,
It is as silent as a grave,
It is as mysterious as
A wizard doing magic.

Michael Blair (8)
St Gabriel's Primary School, Prestonpans

THE COMETS

C   omets
O   n the moon,
M   eeting each other, they are
E   xtremely
T   ired now,
S   ome are red and some are yellow.

Lucy Johnson (8)
St Gabriel's Primary School, Prestonpans

SPACE

Space is like a big open sea
It is as dark as black paint
It is as silent as stars twinkling
It is as mysterious as a mystery
It is 89 suns put together
It is cold as a cucumber
It is as inviting as a tea party.

Nicole Cunningham (7)
St Gabriel's Primary School, Prestonpans

FIREWORK NIGHT

On firework night
I stand at the window
And stare and stare and stare
At the things that are
Out there
In the thin, thin, thin
Thin air
I do like Hallowe'en
I do like Christmas time
But my favourite time of all
Would be sparkly
Firework night.

Ciara Gracie (8)
St Joseph's Primary School, Linlithgow

THE RAIN AND THE RAINBOW

I am sitting in my room
And I am wondering
When will the sun come out?
It's pouring down with rain
And I can't go outside
Because of that
So I watched the television
And I got fed up with it
So I went up to my room
But then the rain stopped
And I went outside
And there was a rainbow
A lovely rainbow.

Lewis Carr (8)
St Joseph's Primary School, Linlithgow

BIRDS, BIRDS

Birds, birds, beautiful birds,
They sing tweet, tweet when the sun
Goes down.
Some people think it is sweet and nice.
Some think it is annoying and horrible.
But I think it is wonderful,
And I love it.

Rebecca Shanks (8)
St Joseph's Primary School, Linlithgow

THE ASTRONAUT

One day I had a dream,
A dream that no one had ever seen.
It was about an astronaut who went to space,
Who went to space at quite a fast pace.
First the astronaut went to the moon,
He went to the moon with his spoon.
He used his spoon to whack an alien on the head,
To whack an alien on the head until the alien was dead.
Next the astronaut went to Mars,
He went to Mars and then the stars.
Then he went to the planet of guitars.
The astronaut said, 'Why don't I take a guitar home,
Because I live in a place called Rome?'
So the astronaut went back to Italy
And everyone cheered there.
Hip hip hooray!

Philip McLean (8)
St Joseph's Primary School, Linlithgow

THE TOSS

There was once a king who ruled his country
And married a queen who like a bounty.
The king loved his country but the queen did not.
The king thought that if they did a toss this would settle it.
So they settled to do a toss.
If it was heads the queen would rule with a different man.
If it was tails the king would rule with a different woman.
So they tossed.
It landed on tails.
The queen was very sad.

Bryon Anderson (8)
St Joseph's Primary School, Linlithgow

THE SHINING MOON

Every night I sit
And watch the moon,
The moon
The lovely shining moon.
The hours go by,
Tick, tick, tick, tick.
The clock strikes twelve,
The moon has gone,
Bye-bye moon
I call, I call,
Then back it comes,
So sweet and soft.
The voice of the moon,
The moon,
Saying next time,
Next time.
Come back, come back,
Come back I cry.
But no, she's gone,
The lovely shining moon has gone.
So I shut the window,
Close the curtains,
Climb into bed
And fall asleep
And dream a lovely dream.

Katherine Orr (8)
St Joseph's Primary School, Linlithgow

MY WINDOW AT NIGHT

Once I saw a light
Shining in the night.
I thought it was quite bright
For an ordinary light.

Just then I saw a thief
Wearing a victor's wreath.
He was an army chief
Eating a piece of beef.

Robyn Brown (8)
St Joseph's Primary School, Linlithgow

COCO THE CIRCUS CLOWN

There was a clown called Coco
That's true
He makes everyone laugh
Me and you
Everyone loves him
They laugh, chuckle
And giggle too
He, he, ho, ho
And ha, ha too
Come on Coco
We love you
You make us laugh and sing Coco
You're the king!
You take string in your hand
And they turn to sand
No more magic
No, no! Coco sing!
Now the show's over
Ooch we cry
Then Coco sings goodbye.

Stephanie Kelly (8)
St Joseph's Primary School, Linlithgow

THE MAGIC BAG

I will put in my bag,
The cheer of the crowd
When the ball hits the net.
The last breath of a lion
And the gleam of gold from a coin.

I will put in my bag,
The first snowflake of a new year.
A black sun and a green fox
And the rarest diamond in the world.

I will put in my bag,
The heartstrings of a dragon,
The rolling eye of a snake
And then I will crawl into the bag
And it will take me to the deepest part of the sea.

My bag is made from
The wool of a golden fleece
And the silk of a solid silver spider.

Patrick Scott (10)
St Joseph's Primary School, Linlithgow

GOD'S LOVE

God's love is blue
Because the sea is blue.
God's love will wash over me
Just like the sea.

God's love is silver
His love is rich.
He gives me everything
And I'm as wealthy as a king.

God's love is grey
When my thoughts are grey.
God will come and
Help me on my way.

Jamie Settle (9)
St Joseph's Primary School, Linlithgow

THE STORM

There once was a storm
A windy storm
That blew the people away.
It made a noise
And whistled like this,
'Wh . . . ooo . . . ooo!'
It blew down a fence
It blew down some trees
It blew down windows
It blew away bees
The storm shook the lights
The flickering lights
It blew off roofs
Some people died
And some got blown away
Children were told not to play
It was a very bad storm
A storm! A storm!
It was a very bad storm.

Beth Corrigan (8)
St Joseph's Primary School, Linlithgow

GOD'S LOVE

God's love is silver
Because the stars are silver
They shine down on you
We know God's love is true.

God's love is black
Because the night is black
When we safely sleep
We know we're in God's keep.

God's love is yellow
Because the sun is yellow
It shines on everything
And it makes the angels sing.

Craig McNee (8)
St Joseph's Primary School, Linlithgow

THE RAINBOW

There once was a rainbow
A very colourful rainbow
It was so silly
It was so dumb
It said bye-bye
When something came by
And it said hello
When they went away
How silly can you get today
It came up before the rain
It went down again after the rain
Again and again.

Matthew McLean (8)
St Joseph's Primary School, Linlithgow

GOD'S LOVE

God's love is blue
Because the sea is blue
As it splashes in and out
We can play and we can shout.

God's love is green
Because the grass is green
God has made the Earth bright
With grass which looks just right.

God's love is brown
Because the bark of trees is brown
They grow up big and strong
With branches for birds to sing a song.

Sean Graham (9)
St Joseph's Primary School, Linlithgow

GOD'S LOVE

God's love is gold
Because the sun is gold
It melts the winter snow
And helps the crops to grow.

God's love is blue
Because the sea is blue
As children splash in and out
While mums and dads shout.

God's love is white
Because snowdrops are white
They shiver in the snow
And make God's love show.

Joanne MacArthur (9)
St Joseph's Primary School, Linlithgow

GOD'S LOVE

God's love is blue
Because the sea is blue
We can splash and play
By it all the day.

God's love is orange
Because fire is orange
Fires keep us warm
Through a winter's storm.

God's love is silver
Because the stars are silver
They shine at night
Like God's love that's bright.

Rachel Moran (9)
St Joseph's Primary School, Linlithgow

GOD'S LOVE

God's love is black
Because the night is black
That is when we sleep
As Jesus guards his sheep.

God's love is blue
Because the sky is blue
God gives us beautiful birds that fly
High above in the bright blue sky.

God's love is yellow
Because the sun is yellow
God created the sun
So we can go out and have great fun.

Daniel McCormack (9)
St Joseph's Primary School, Linlithgow

GOD'S LOVE

God's love is blue
Because the sea is blue
It splashes all day
And in it we can play.

God's love is orange
Because the sun is orange
It shines all day
So we can see our way.

God's love is silver
Because the stars are silver
They brighten the sky with fairy lights
So we can dance all night.

Paul Keane (9)
St Joseph's Primary School, Linlithgow

GOD'S LOVE

God's love is blue
Because the sky is blue
It covers us all
Whether we're big or small.

God's love is orange
Because fruit is orange
It's good and sweet
For girls and boys to eat.

God's love is brown
Because soil is brown
It helps the plants to grow
Whether it's rain or snow.

Stephanie Duffy (9)
St Joseph's Primary School, Linlithgow

GOD'S LOVE

God's love is gold
Because the sun is gold
It helps the crops to grow
And melts the icy snow.

God's love is red
Our school uniform is red
At school God helps us learn
And he gets us through the term.

God's love is silver
Because the stars are silver
God makes the night
And it sparkles with parts of light.

Rosie Barron (9)
St Joseph's Primary School, Linlithgow

GOD'S LOVE

God's love is brown
Because our house is brown
It shelters us from rain
So we don't feel any pain.

God's love is orange
Because the sun is orange
It shines on everything
And makes the angels sing.

God's love is silver
Because the stars are silver
They make the night bright
By shining lots of light.

Erin Tierney (9)
St Joseph's Primary School, Linlithgow

GOD'S LOVE

God's love is blue
Because it feels true.
It blows through our hearts
It makes us feel like we're number one in the charts
He loves us for who we are.

God's love is silver
Because coins are silver
But God's love is more valuable
God's love is silver
Like twinkling stars
They shine over me
Beyond the distant sea.

Amy McDonnell (9)
St Joseph's Primary School, Linlithgow

GOD'S LOVE

God's love is emerald
Because the sea is emerald.
His love washes over me
Like the warm green sea.

God's love is blue
Because the rain is blue.
It waters all the plants
In the wind they all dance.

God's love is red
Like the centre of a candle.
You can light them in the church
If your heart by sadness has been touched.

Ruairidh Patfield (9)
St Joseph's Primary School, Linlithgow

God's Love

God's love is red
Because the sun is red
It gives us light
And makes the whole world bright.

God's love is silver
Like church bells that ring
They call us each day
And help us on our way.

God's love is blue
Like ice in winter
People love to skate
On a happy joyful date.

Eleni Katsoulis (9)
St Joseph's Primary School, Linlithgow

Christmas

C hristmas is coming, snow's falling,
H o, ho, ho! Santa calling.
R eindeers flying
I 'm sighing
S anta's crying, eating his snack
T rying to pack his huge red sack.
M rs Claus is saying goodbye
A s Santa goes away up high.
S houting 'Have a merry Christmas!'

Hayley Cherry (11)
St Mary's RC Primary School, Bonnyrigg

CHRISTMAS

C akes are baking
H ungry children are taking,
R eindeers can fly
I n the frosty sky.
S anta has fun
T aking a bite of his bun.
M ummy's downstairs wrapping toys
A nd only for the girls and boys
S uddenly Santa's off with glee.

Iain Toule (11)
St Mary's RC Primary School, Bonnyrigg

CHRISTMAS

C hristmas won't last
H olly is past
R eindeers will crash
I ce pools will smash
S now is tiny
T rees are shiny
M ary is waiting on her mat
A nna is waiting to play with her bats
S anta's coming, he's running!

Samantha Waugh (11)
St Mary's RC Primary School, Bonnyrigg

DAYDREAMS

Mrs Loughton thinks I'm reading
But I'm an explorer on a ship, looking for treasure
or swimming with whales,
I'm bumping into a sword fish
and against an octopus.
I go home at night
with the treasure I've found in the sea.

Mrs Loughton thinks I'm listening -
But no!
I'm marrying a boy who's at my table
I'm in a boat, rushing through the water
and singing at a concert in Hollywood
I probably broke the windows!

I think of leaving school and getting a job
and running for the navy
or riding a horse in the field.
I go round to my gran's house
and eat steak pie.
When I wake up
I'm covered in sharpenings
My tub has fallen over!

Emma Morley (11)
St Mary's RC Primary School, Bonnyrigg

WHAT IS THE SUN?

The sun is a hot vindaloo without basmati rice,
It is a brandy without the glass.
The sun is the great provider, without the money,
It is a crackling barbecue, without the coals.

The sun is a hot chilli pepper, without the seeds,
It is a campfire without the sausages and marshmallows.
The sun is a guideline without the map,
It is the fire without the hearth,
It is the light of our world.

Fiona Cumberland (11)
St Mary's RC Primary School, Bonnyrigg

DAYDREAMS

Mrs Loughton thinks I'm looking
but I'm really booking
a flight to Japan . . .
I'm getting ready to fire
a crook called Carter Ire . . .
I'm laying the smackdown
on a guy called Joe Layden.

Mrs Loughton thinks I'm reading
but I'm really feeding
a shark from Pakistan . . .
I'm fighting away terrorists
from my lovely school.

Mrs Loughton thinks I'm listening
but I'm really glistening
in a television show . . .
I'm surging on the highway
going really fast,
but now my daydream
is over and I'm now
back in my class.

Christopher Darling (11)
St Mary's RC Primary School, Bonnyrigg

DAYDREAMS

Mrs Loughton thinks I'm reading
But I'm boxing Lennox Lewis and Mike Tyson
beating them in round five
or beating the 100 metres record for running.
I'm dating Jennifer Lopez
or saving people from a plane crash.
I'm getting a medal from the Queen
or throwing millions from the Eiffel Tower.

Mrs Loughton thinks I'm listening
She wishes!
I'm in a sports car
beating Colin Macrae at the Swedish rally course.
I am the world's strongest man
watching a romantic move,
blowing my nose with fifty pound notes
climbing Mount Everest.
Then I woke up because I got a fright
from Mrs Loughton shouting
'Sean, get a Time Out!'

Sean Crawford (11)
St Mary's RC Primary School, Bonnyrigg

TED

I really love to go to bed
And cuddle into my bear Ted
My mum and dad say I'm mad
But I don't think it's all that bad

I like Ted very much
My sister thinks he's going to burst
But Ted is my loveable bear
Who gets tangled in my hair.

Jennifer Kelly (11)
St Mary's RC Primary School, Bonnyrigg

DAYDREAMS

Mrs Loughton thinks I'm writing
but I'm in Hollywood
being a film star, best of the best
or driving a silver car - Lotus preferably . . .
on the long motorway.

Mrs Loughton thinks I'm reading -
but I'm a millionaire, spending money
every day,
or flying in mighty space with aliens
scampering away from me!

Mrs Loughton thinks I'm listening
but I'm an archaeologist searching for
tombs to raid
or scoring thirty goals for Celtic
or even cuddling warm polar bears.
When I wake up
I am amazed -
the classroom is empty.

Daniel Donaldson (11)
St Mary's RC Primary School, Bonnyrigg

DAYDREAMS

Mrs Loughton thinks I'm reading
But I'm sending my monster on a boxer
I am a spy who will not die
I am playing with my toys, making lots of noise
Then I am on holiday
Sitting in the sun

I am an eye looking at the sky
I am at the beach
Trying to teach . . . the fish to swim
I am soaring in the air
Jumping on the clouds

Mrs Loughton thinks I'm listening,
Oh no, I'm not
I am in my own little world
With my monsters and my toys
In the clouds
When I wake up I'm all glue
And Mrs Loughton is too.

Christopher Paul (10)
St Mary's RC Primary School, Bonnyrigg

A LONELY LITTLE TURTLE

A lonely little turtle was lying on the beach,
For years now, he had longed to preach.
All he had on this deserted land
Was the roaring waves and the silky sand.

He didn't have a family,
He didn't have a friend,
He thought that this might be the end!
Until one day, came washing ashore.
A female turtle, whom he came to adore.

Emma Duffy (11)
St Mary's RC Primary School, Bonnyrigg

DAYDREAM

Mrs Loughton thinks I'm reading.
Never!
I'm the most famous singer in the world
and I'm singing live on MTV.
Or dancing behind J Lo at her concert.
I won 'Who Wants To Be a Millionaire'
And I'm the richest person in the world.
I've married Brad Pitt,
and I've bought a huge mansion
and now I'm splashing in the big pool.

Mrs Loughton thinks I'm listening.
Never!
I'm in the Atlantic Ocean, drowning on the Titanic,
but here comes my hero, Leonardo de Caprio.
Or I've found the necklace with the blue diamond.

Then I wake up . . .
For some reason my
Whole class are laughing!

Oriana Andreucci (11)
St Mary's RC Primary School, Bonnyrigg

DAYDREAMS

Mrs Loughton thinks I'm reading
Yeah, right! I'm in a boxing club
or the world's 25m jumping competition.
I am the world's Irish Dancing champion
or swimming in the 1,000m race.

Mrs Loughton thinks I'm listening
Sure!
I'm filming Robbie Williams in his boxing shorts
or the first and only person to be a millionaire.
I am the best player for tennis,
or even basketball.

'Siobhan!'
'Sorry, just had a *daydream!'*

Siobhan Mulvey (11)
St Mary's RC Primary School, Bonnyrigg

WHAT IS THE SUN?

The sun is a firework without the bang,
It is a cream cake without the cream.
The sun is a baby spice without the spice,
It is a burning meteor without the rock.
The sun is a liquid without the water,
It is a candle without the wax.
The sun is a voice circle without the voice.
It is my best friend without the silliness.
The sun is a lighter without the gas,
It is the lamp without the shade.

Michelle Ramage Hall (11)
St Mary's RC Primary School, Bonnyrigg

WHAT IS THE SUN?

The sun is a burning light without the light shade
It is a huge great star without the shine,
The sun is a round ball without the bounce
It is a bright orange without the juice.
The sun is a button without the shine
The sun is a flag without the flick.
It is like a big yellow ball without the shape.
The sun is a fag without the smoke
It is a huge star without the shine.

Jacqueline Ferrell (11)
St Mary's RC Primary School, Bonnyrigg

CHRISTMAS

C hristmas is coming
H eavy snow is falling
R eindeer are flying
I n the workshop Santa is prying
S anta eats a bit of a tart
T hat Rudolph waits for a part
M any people play in the snow
A nd they do a pantomime show
S anta is coming to town.

Ross Dickson (11)
St Mary's RC Primary School, Bonnyrigg

About My Rabbit

Fit . . . goes to football training
Runs about madly!
He is mental
He's cute and furry
He's a great rabbit.
He might be small and big-eared
But he's still my rabbit.
I love him
Floppy is cool
He can walk and talk
He's funky
I've had three other rabbits before

My first one was Sneaky
Second one was Floppy
Third one was Ernie . . .
But Floppy is the best!

Stephanie Grant (10)
St Peter's Primary School, Dumbarton

The Sun

The sun is shining
As warm as the fire in the house
As good as a rocket
As liked as games
As welcome as my mum
As needed as toys
I like the sun.

Robbie Cockerell (10)
St Peter's Primary School, Dumbarton

I DON'T LIKE THE DARK

When I go to bed
I hear creaks
I look back
I can't see anything
I see shadows
I look back
I see nothing
I hear the TV
I feel frightened
I hear dogs barking
In the streets
I hear noises under
My bed, terrified
I don't like the dark.

John Rylance (10)
St Peter's Primary School, Dumbarton

THE SUN

The sun is
As warm as toast roasted by
A log fire
As good as a strawberry milkshake
As liked as your friends
As welcome as a party
As needed as your mum and dad
I like the sun

Daniel Millar (10)
St Peter's Primary School, Dumbarton

DREAMING

Am I dreaming or is this real?
It feels like I'm in a magic land.
Wind with gold dust passes my face,
Unicorns are galloping by,
Enchanted music fills the air.
Close by a phoenix cries pearl tears.
I feel so light and airy . . .
Then I come down with a bump.

It is the wind.

You cannot see it
Unless it beats against the tree
Or when it glides softly over your face
Or moves your hair all over the place.

Then I know for sure.

It is real
And not a dream.

Heather Doran (11)
St Peter's Primary School, Dumbarton

NOODLES

I love noodles -
Ra! Ra! Ra!
But I don't like poodles -
Na! Na! Na!
Feet smell yuck,
My finger is stuck,
But do I like noodles?
Ya! Ya! Ya!

Jennifer Sayer (11)
St Peter's Primary School, Dumbarton

ANIMALS

Cunning as the tiger
Who slips through the grass,
Cute as the elephant
With their huge flapping ears,
Hyenas are skinny and gangly
And snakes eat eggs and rats,
Monkeys are sweet
Swinging like a yo-yo,
Wolves are scary
And can be vicious too,
Dogs are soft and cuddly
Crocs are nasty and envious,
Kittens are cute and lazy
Fish are horrible and scaly,
But rabbits with their soft fur
Is why I like them
The best.

Jayne Faickney (11)
St Peter's Primary School, Dumbarton

MY GOLDFISH

Swim around in their tank
Round and round they go
They chase each other
night and day
I think they need some food just to last the year.
They chase,
Sleep
But they always stay awake!
They are Harvey and Sabrina -
My loveable fish.

Kayleigh McMillan (11)
St Peter's Primary School, Dumbarton

MY PET GOLDFISH

I have a goldfish
She is my pet
She is never dry
She is always wet

She can do a cool trick
And jump out of the water
It is so brilliant
Because I taught her

I am so glad that I
Bought her -
My pet goldfish

Nicholas Kane (11)
St Peter's Primary School, Dumbarton

WHEN IT IS DARK

When I was in my bed
Feeling relaxed
I shut my eyes
For two minutes!
I heard a howling
I began to feel scared
I decided to ignore it -
And then I fell asleep!

Monica Slaven (10)
St Peter's Primary School, Dumbarton

THE SUN

As good as the scarf which goes
around my neck
As good as birthday toys
As liked as party food
As welcome as a birthday boy
As needed as the money we buy things with
I like the sun.

David Henderson (10)
St Peter's Primary School, Dumbarton

THE SUN

The sun is
As warm as a log fire
As good as a new toy
As liked as a new baby
As welcomed as a new friend
As needed as food
I love the sun!

Andrew Gilmour (9)
St Peter's Primary School, Dumbarton

HOLIDAY

H olidays
O n the caves
L azy ways
I n a daze
D oing the craze
A fter the ways
Y our lazy days

James Maloney (11)
St Peter's Primary School, Dumbarton

THE SUN

As warm as a hot fire
As good as a toy
As liked as a boy
As welcome as water
As needed as heat
I like the sun

Ross Laughland (9)
St Peter's Primary School, Dumbarton

THE SUN

The sun is as bright as Heaven
As warm as a demon mad
As good as games
As liked as a toy
As needed as food
I like the sun.

Graeme Biggins (10)
St Peter's Primary School, Dumbarton

RAIN

Oh no!
Raining again,
Always the same.

Plop, plop, plop, plops the rain,
Filling up the gutters with ice-cold water.

Rumble, rumble, rumble sounds the thunder,
As loud as gunshots fired in a round.

I feel cold, horrid, bored,
And the rain patters on the windowpane.
Patter, patter, patter.

I can't get outside,
There's nothing to do,
It's boring inside.

Becky McTaggart (11)
Southend Primary School, Campbeltown

RAIN

Rain is falling from the sky,
Tears from the sky fall down on me,
And all the gutters fill up.

The water is creating muddy puddles
So I jump in them and get wet,
The rain falls down
Like an upside-down bucket of water.

Drops of rain make noises on the windows,
Eating our lunch we hear the rain,
And if you go outside, you'll get wet!

Eilidh McLaughlin (11)
Southend Primary School, Campbeltown

RAIN

Children jumping and splashing in puddles,
I jump into my coat and run outside.

Boom, bang, goes the thunder,
Flash, flash, goes the lightning.

The rain clatters and patters on my coat,
Suddenly the wind picks up.

The clatter of bins rushing through the street,
Trees swaying in every direction.

Drip, drip, drip, goes the water down a drain.
I sprint as fast as a cheetah into the house,
I whip off my wet clothes.

I make hot chocolate with marshmallows,
And sit by the fire with a comic.
Brrr! Chilly.

I hope it's not like this on sports day.

Aidan Thomson (11)
Southend Primary School, Campbeltown

RAIN

Splosh! Splash!
I jump in the puddles.
I like to get soaked and jump about.

People are rushing up and down the street
Like wet dogs.
The rain rushes down the drains,
They can't take much more.

The streets are spotted with umbrellas.
I feel cold, but happy,
I hear people saying how terrible it is
But I like it.

Back inside,
The rain runs down the window.

Kenneth Galbraith (11)
Southend Primary School, Campbeltown

RAIN

It's raining.
I go outside,
Get on my bike,
Go like the wind!
And splash through puddles.
Splash! Splash! Splashes the rain.
I am soaked.
Mum shouts, 'Come in now!'
But I carry on sploshing.
By the time I come in
My clothes are soaking
And my boots are full of water.
When the rain stops
I go outside again.
Mum says, 'Don't get wet!'
But it's no fun
Not getting wet.

Craig McKerral (10)
Southend Primary School, Campbeltown

RAIN!

It starts to rain,
'Oh yes!' I say,
All I can hear is *pitter-patter, pitter-patter,*
Inside I feel an urge to go outside
And jump in the puddles,
Outside I go *splish, splash, splish!*
I can only see puddles,
I start to count them,
1, 2, 3 *splash!* 5, 6, 7 *splash!*
I go back inside and get dried,
Out of the window I can see,
Other children jumping in puddles,
The rain is dying down now,
Then it stops.
It had been raining
Like it had never rained before.

Kerri McCorkindale (10)
Southend Primary School, Campbeltown

RAIN

It's raining again
Oh! What a splatter!
Started off sunny
and now it's a clatter.
It's falling down
like heavy rocks
but then it changes
into blocks.

Bang! goes a streak
of lightning,
thud is the sound
of the thunder biting.
Then comes nightfall
it still is raining.
I think it was a flood
there's a dragged wet canine.

Matthew Hales (11)
Southend Primary School, Campbeltown

RAIN

Drip, drop, drip, drop,
The rain on the windowpane.

Pitter-patter, pitter-patter,
As the rain hits the roof,
Like a horse's hoof on stone.

Splish, splash! Splish, splash!
As a car drives by,
Sending a puddle over the kerb,
Like a tidal wave sweeping over the ground.

Gush, gash! Gush, gash!
The rain disappears down the drain,
Like the water tumbling over
The edge of a waterfall.

Fraser Cameron (11)
Southend Primary School, Campbeltown

RAIN

Splish, splash goes the rain on the window,
People run home in a rush.

Boom, boom, thunder echoes in the streets,
The sky lights up like a spark.

Drip, drop, drip, drop,
Children jumping in puddles.

I count them, 1, 2, 3, s*plash!*
Someone falls in.

All I can hear is the rain dying down,
The sky clears up and I'm happy,
The sun is back out again.

Jennifer Galbraith (11)
Southend Primary School, Campbeltown

RAIN

It's raining.
Out of the window
People run to their cars,
Children splash in puddles.

'Granny it's raining,' I say.
'My washing!' she shrieks.
We run to the car . . .

When we get home
Granny grabs the washing.
It's soaking,
She shoves it in the tumble-dryer.

Karen Semple (10)
Southend Primary School, Campbeltown

Rain

It's cold and it's pouring down,
Like a waterfall in the summer,
Bobbing umbrellas
Up and down,
Like rubber ducks in a bath tub.
Cars passing,
Splashing the pavement,
Like waves hitting the shore.
Drip, drip, down my back,
As we pass a broken gutter.
Splash, splash on the road,
As it forms a nice small puddle.
I'm cold and wet,
If I was wrung out,
I could fill a whole sink with water!

Susan Houston (11)
Southend Primary School, Campbeltown

My Birthday

I can't wait until my birthday,
I will turn a different age,
Then I will be older than I used to be,
I will get more responsibility than I ever had before,
Now I'm looking to the year ahead,
So now that I have grown up a little,
I will be able to do more things,
So I hope all my wishes come true.

Sindy Urban (11)
Stobhill Primary School, Gorebridge

THE SANDS OF TIME

I walk across the moonlit beach
Humming along with the waves,
As they splash upon the white sand
Like paint spraying onto a white piece of paper.
I gaze up to the starry sky
And believe that I'm in Heaven,
Lighting each star like a candle.
I sit down on a rock,
Running my fingers through my hair
Like a beautiful mermaid would.
I reach down
And take a million grains of sand,
Letting them slip through my fingers
Like the sands of time,
Just as I have done
In this white moonlit heaven.

Rachel Quinn (11)
Stobhill Primary School, Gorebridge

ONE DARK NIGHT

One dark, dark night,
In a dark, dark castle,
Lay a dark, dark dog,
In front of a dark, dark door.

Behind that dark, dark door
Was a dark, dark shadow,
Behind that dark, dark shadow
Was a dark, dark box.

And in that dark, dark box
Was two dark, dark eyes,
From a dark, dark face
With a dark, dark mouth.

And from that dark, dark mouth
Came a dark, dark voice.
The dark, dark voice said,
'Will someone put the lights on,
It's dark in here!'

Amy Young (11)
Stobhill Primary School, Gorebridge

LITTLE RABBIT

O, wee rabbit,
You must be tired,
Day after day getting chased,
My dog nearly caught you,
Run rabbit run,
In and out, Spike's legs,
Up and down the hill,
Missed you by 1cm,
He's lost you now,
Oh no, here come Dillan,
Run to the woods,
Look out, Spike's coming back,
Same routine again,
Run home rabbit,
See you soon.

Loretta Flanagan (11)
Stobhill Primary School, Gorebridge

TWA WEE BUDGIES

Twa wee budgies,
Sittin' in a cage,
Yin wis yelli,
Yin wis baidge,
Yin hud a wee beak,
Yin hud a long tail,
Yin hud a wee tae,
Yin hud nun at o,
So there ye huv,
Twa wee budgies,
Sittin' in a cage,
Yin wis yelli,
An yin wis definitely baidge.

Danielle Robinson (10)
Stobhill Primary School, Gorebridge

MY SISTER

I hate my sister,
She is a pain,
I love my sister all the same.
She makes a mess,
I clean it up.
She makes a noise,
I say shut up.
But she's my sister
I wouldn't give her up.

Sarah Donaghy (11)
Stobhill Primary School, Gorebridge

GUESS WHAT?

I have two wheels,
I like to go fast,
I have a metal frame
With handlebars,
And my seat is padded.
I have travelled around the world.
I have been on television.
I have won four championships.
The colour of me is red.
My name is Carl Fogarty.

Can you guess what I do?
Can you guess what I am?
Can you guess what type of machine I ride?

Stewart Pearson (11)
Stobhill Primary School, Gorebridge

MY BOX OF TREASURES

In my box of treasures I have
A magic map that takes me to different worlds,
Worlds of mystery that could make you scared.
With my pencils and felt tips
I can invent new countries and worlds.
These worlds are locked up where
I can open them any time
And let them out.

Grant Gibson (8)
Strachur Primary School, Cairndow

MY TREASURE BOX

In my box of treasures
I have . . .
A beautiful diamond ring
That helps me to remember my days
When I was little.

In my box of treasures
I have . . .
A w
    a
     t
      e
       r
        f
         a
          l
           l
From a beautiful walk on a summer's day.

In my box of treasures
I have . . .
A twinkling star I saved from France
And a memory of freedom and laughter.

Eilidh MacRaild (8)
Strachur Primary School, Cairndow

MY TREASURE BOX

In my box of treasures
Are the voices of the world,
Ferocious voices, kind voices,
Evil voices and good,
Whirling voices, twirling voices,
Voices that want to get out.

Mum's voice and Dad's voice,
Voices of all my friends
Wizards' voices and spellbinding
Witches' voices that turn me into a frog
But best of all my favourite voice is my own,
My own personal one.

Tom Adrian (9)
Strachur Primary School, Cairndow

COOL DRAGON

There is a cool dragon inside me
That makes me go out and party all night.

There is a cool dragon inside me
That makes me behave in class.

There is a clean dragon inside me
That makes me have baths all the time.

There is a soft dragon inside me
That makes me cuddle up to my toys.

There is a funny dragon inside me
That makes me giggle.

There is a forgettable dragon inside me
That makes me forget everything.

There is a . . . oh dear, I've forgotten!

Elizabeth Pope (9)
Strachur Primary School, Cairndow

THE DRAGON INSIDE ME

There is a horrid dragon inside me
That makes me kick people with my very hard boots
And makes them scream and yell.
There is a cruel dragon inside me
That makes me stand on people's toes in the line and laugh at them.
There is a rude dragon inside me
That makes me make rude noises in assembly.
There is a nasty dragon inside me
That makes me tell on people when they didn't do anything.
There is an uncontrollable dragon inside me
That makes me stand on tables and chairs -
Then the teacher comes and I am in serious trouble.
There is an ugly dragon inside me
That makes me scribble all over the work that I did.

Iain-Hamish Paton (9)
Strachur Primary School, Cairndow

MY BOX OF TREASURES

In my box of treasures
I have a magical mirror.
This mirror can tell me how to do my housework
And how to make a clay house.
It can make me fly right up to the moon
And take me onto a cloud.
Quick! I must wrap it up in this silk cloth,
And place it gently back in the big red box.

Zoe Hempleman (8)
Strachur Primary School, Cairndow

MY BOX OF TREASURES

In my box of treasures
I have a dazzling pearl,
A lucky coin
And the sun,
Oh look how it sparkles in the sky,
It makes me feel like I am in Heaven.
Oh, and best of all
I have a crystal ball.
The crystal ball
Can make me fly.
I play hide-and-seek with the clouds,
I look down and see
All the children playing.
Then I wrap my dreams in the box
And open the box again.

Hazel Hunter (8)
Strachur Primary School, Cairndow

ME

My hair is like needles threaded with silk.
My eyes are the colour of cannonballs.
My teeth are like plaster.
My tongue is like popcorn bubbling.
My fingers are like ammo.
My legs are like walking sticks in action.
My feet are like matchsticks burning to run.
My toes are like wires sparkling.

Alistair Clark (8)
Strachur Primary School, Cairndow

IN MY BOX OF TREASURES

In my box of treasures I found
A pair of earrings,
Sparkling, magical earrings,
Not just any old pair.
A note was lying beside them -
'Hi! Keep these earrings!'
Amazed and astonished
I gazed at the diamonds in the middle
Flashing with rainbow-coloured waves around it.
The colours blended together,
I kept them forever.

Linda Robertson (9)
Strachur Primary School, Cairndow

MY BOX OF TREASURES

In my box of treasures
Lies my magic medal.
When I ask, it will reply.
It will take me where I wish to go.
It will get me what I want to have,
And tell me about the past.
It can make me do magic
And fly in the air.
It can take me to magical lands
Where I see the most amazing things.

Rory MacLachlan (8)
Strachur Primary School, Cairndow

WAITING

I am so bored
That I start to daydream,
I fiddle with my pencils,
My face droops,
My eyes fall out of their sockets,
I bite my nails,
I feel brain-dead
Like a headless chicken,
A zombie awakening from the dead.

Andrew Wilson (9)
Strachur Primary School, Cairndow

SAD WITCH

The horrible, scary witch
Has a green nose
And a hideous appearance.
She likes to pose
And be an interference.
She likes to eat children
And roast beef with mud,
But I don't think she likes ice cream - sad!

Naomi Sturrock (8)
Strachur Primary School, Cairndow

NEVER GO NEAR A DRAGON

D ozy, dainty dragon,
R aging, roaring, really fierce,
A nimals beware killer,
G anging dragon, goblins' friend,
O vergrown, meat-loving,
N ever go near a dragon.

Laura Campbell (8)
Strachur Primary School, Cairndow

DEMON DRAGON

D iamonds cover his demons,
R ich, roaring dragon,
A mazed by his shining skin,
G rumpy, grinning dragon,
O oooh, his shine, ooooh his grumps,
N o one likes dragons.

Katie McNair (9)
Strachur Primary School, Cairndow

TREASURE

In my box of treasures
I have a beautiful diamond ring.
It is a fantastic shiny ring,
It has a brilliant stone inside it.
Best of all it is in the safest box
You can ever buy.

Karin Reid (9)
Strachur Primary School, Cairndow

TEACHERS

Teachers, teachers,
What do they do?
When they are angry their faces turn blue!

Some teachers are nice,
But some are not.
There is a stinkbomb,
Nah, I'd better not!

They make us do loads and loads of work,
I'm glad I'm in such a small school
With not much homework!

Karen Mayberry (9)
Toward Primary School, Dunoon

MY FRIEND GOBLIN

I've got a friend named Goblin,
He's smaller than a hen.
Even though he scares me,
He's still my very best friend.
People think he's ugly and stupid,
But he's smart enough to do a quiz.
Even if he's very ugly
I like him just the way he is.

William Stirling (9)
Toward Primary School, Dunoon

HOMEWORK

Homework is what all pupils hate,
The teachers give it at such a rate.
When homework's given we all give a groan,
Though the teachers say, 'There's no need to moan!'

PE is a subject I really don't mind,
For homework my teacher, he never can find!

Now French and English I really can't do,
They just seem to get me right into a stew.

Geography is a subject I really despise,
And when we get homework it's mainly to revise.

History is a class that's really a bore,
When I think I've learnt everything there always is more.

Maths is a subject I really detest,
By the time I have started I'm needing a rest!

Science is a class which I really can't stand,
For it seems, always, my teacher has a homework demand.

The one thing in common that homework's all got,
Is that pupils can't stand it, they hate it the lot!

Elspeth MacDonald (10)
Toward Primary School, Dunoon

GHOSTS UNITED

They can walk through a wall,
But can't kick a ball.

The fans start screaming,
The players' eyes are gleaming.

The fans are humming,
'Ghosts United'.

The players wonder why,
As they're at the bottom of the Spooky League.

Ian Dornan (11)
Toward Primary School, Dunoon

GHOSTS

Ghosts are scary!
They are bright.
They are very white
And they lurk in the deepest corners.

They can walk through a wall
And you can hear them call
Your name!
People think you're insane.

Ghosts will haunt you!
They will kill too!
Writhing in pain on the floor
You shout for him to stop,
But he simply says, 'You deserve more!'

You walk home
And tell your friends,
But they laugh and say,
'What next? A gnome?'

David Stirling (11)
Toward Primary School, Dunoon

HIDDEN TREASURE

Hidden treasure so they say,
Is lying somewhere in the bay.
A Spanish galleon it is told,
Is full of precious gems and gold.
This vessel smashed upon the rocks,
'Abandon ship!' cried out the cox.
The sailors managed to swim ashore,
The treasure lost for ever more.
Gold and gems beneath the sea,
Now lost for eternity.

Michael Thomson (11)
Toward Primary School, Dunoon

PIE

I love pie,
I make it all the time.
No one can tell me a lie about pie!
Pie is so sweet,
It's all I can eat.
I can't eat sausages because they are so saucy.
I can't eat chips because they are so crunchy.
I can't eat currie because it nips my lips.
All I can eat is pie, sweet pie,
And that's no lie!

Lynsey Walker (10)
Troon Primary School, Troon

TELETUBBIE DAVID

My friend David is a Teletubbie,
He is very short and stubby.
I know this is really sad,
But David's hair is really bad.
The bit that sticks up makes him look like Tinky Winky,
And his breath is really stinky.
Now his breath is not that bad,
But I still think I am being sad.
He is really good at golf,
But when he gets a cold his nose is like Rudolf.
His wee sister Laura is really cool,
In fact all his family really rule.
I've stayed over at his place before,
The only thing wrong is his awful snore.

Douglas Steele (11)
Troon Primary School, Troon

LIKE A ROSE

Like a rose am I,
Bright when the sun is out,
As the sun is my friend.

Like a rose am I,
In the rain,
Heavy with water, my roots are soaked.

Like a rose am I,
Bright and beautiful,
Like a rose am I.

Nicola Carter (10)
Troon Primary School, Troon

CHRISTMAS!

It was the night before Christmas
And all through the house
Every creature was stirring, even the mouse.
But I was asleep in my bed, *not!*
Did you think I'd forgotten . . .
  Christmas?
I ran to a room to wake up my brother,
Then I went downstairs to wake up my mother.
In my mum and dad's room I jumped on the bed,
I accidentally hit my dad on the head.
He woke up with a groan,
My mum woke up with a moan.
  It's Christmas!
I opened all my toys,
Got some deodorant (just for boys).
I got some CDs and a CD player,
My dad was surprised to get a DVD player.
  Christmas!
Later that day I had tea with my gran,
With my aunt and my cousins, my mum was going mad!
My grandad and dad started to squeal,
How could they watch TV while eating a meal?
Eventually my mum slapped them in the side,
'Get to the table, get off your backside!'
  Christmas!
That night I went to my bed
With a very good feeling and a good thought in my head.
  Christmas!

Neil G Currie (10)
Troon Primary School, Troon

THE DOLPHIN

I met a dolphin the other day
Swimming up and down the bay,
Gliding past the seaweed
That got in her way.

Every time I see that dolphin
I feel a strange feeling,
Like I want to swim with her,
In the clear blue sea.

That night I dreamt I was swimming with her
Up and down the bay,
In and out of rocks and seaweed,
Gliding all the way.

I called the dolphin Whisky,
She is bright and very frisky,
Swimming and gliding
With gleaming skin.

At last it's time to go home,
Whisky and I swim back to the shore.
I said goodbye and waved to her,
Then with a flick of her tail she was gone.

I go and see Whisky every day,
She makes me laugh to see her play.
Now this is where the poem ends,
Ps - I got to swim with a dolphin!

Lauren Cole (11)
Troon Primary School, Troon

BERNARD LANGER

Bernard Langer bought an old scrappy banger
An Austin Healey that could do a ten feet wheelie
With rubbish brakes and a million mistakes
He had to eat ten fat steaks

With Bernard Langer and his banger
Along with Gary and his Ferrari and Bill with his Porsche
It didn't look good when they went out for a meal and had
a main course

And that's the story of Bernard Langer
And his old scrappy banger Langer.

James Stewart Hall (10)
Troon Primary School, Troon

A FRIEND

A friend is someone who is there when you need them,
And doesn't care if you play a game and beat them.
They swap games and toys,
And when they're together they make tonnes of noise.
They play football and go skating down the shore,
They have some dinner and then shout for more.
All that fun ends soon,
When one of you moves house,
You say your final goodbyes and start to cry.
The car starts, so you get in,,
And you never look back.
'Those were the best years of my life,' mumbled Jack.

Keir Marshall (11)
Troon Primary School, Troon

GIRL PROBLEMS

There's a blonde-haired girl I kind of like,
She has sea-blue eyes and she sits on the far right.
Her hair waves all the way down to her shoulders,
She's so fit she could fight with soldiers.

When she puts her hand through her hair I quiver,
And when I see her with someone else it's like a stabbing
pain in my liver.

I'm too afraid to ask her out,
In case she rejects me with a loud no.

I'm scared to be around her in case I muck up,
If I eat chocolate I'll cough it back up,
And I found out today I love her.

Christopher Galloway (11)
Troon Primary School, Troon

THE SIMPSONS

I love The Simpsons, my favourite is Homer,
He's got friends so he is not a loner.
Homer is really lazy, his family are all crazy.
Now Bart, he's really funny, all his family are cool,
The problem is that they aren't very rich, they don't have a pool.
Lisa is really smart and Bart is really dumb,
Maggie is young so she sucks her thumb.
You could mistake Marge's hair as a bush,
Nelson the bully has to always punch and push.

The Simpsons is the greatest TV programme ever.

Scott Irvine (11)
Troon Primary School, Troon

THE THING

I don't know what he is for sure
But he creeps around each night
Creeping into houses
Giving people frights

You can't see him because he's invisible
But you know when he's there
There's a shiver up your spine as he goes past
When you turn and there's nothing there

I don't think he's friendly
He's really very nasty
I don't know what he eats
But he stole my chicken pastie

I used to be scared of him
As you can see
But now he's just a gust of wind
That's just a mist
                    Or is he?

Jessica Knox (11)
Troon Primary School, Troon

HAMSTERS

I used to have a hamster,
I loved him very much.
He was very cute and cuddly,
And lovely and soft to touch.

He always loved to play
And run around the floor.
He chewed at everything,
Even my bedroom door!

My hamster's name was Lucky,
He was a really lovely boy.
Everybody liked him,
And his special toy.

Fiona Dobbie (11)
Troon Primary School, Troon

HORSES

Horses are my favourite animals
They like to gallop around the field
Eating long blades of grass
Munching at their will.

Banging on their door
Waiting for their hay
Horses like to eat all day

Put on their saddle
Tighten up their girth
Slide on their bridle
Ready for work

Jump up
Walk them round and round
Trot, canter
Finally jump

Bring them in
Muck them out
Fill up their haynets
Mix up their feeds

Go home after a long day.

Lorna Aitken (11)
Troon Primary School, Troon

DRAGON BALL Z

There once was a bad boy called Cell,
He hit and kicked all the boys and girls.
Then came a good guy named Gohan,
He hit and attacked him with a frying pan.

Cell was knocked out with a broken leg,
Then the hero Gohan said,
'The pain you're feeling is the pain you gave,
Now I'll send you to your grave.'

Gohan killed Cell with a blast,
Now he is sent back to the past.
He will go down to Hell.
Thank the Lord the world's saved from Cell.

Everyone will throw a party for Gohan,
As he's the one who hit Cell with a frying pan.
He is the world's strongest boy,
Now everyone's happy and full of joy!

Andrew Coll (11)
Troon Primary School, Troon

ELEPHANTS

Elephants walk about eating leaves
They take them from huge trees
At the end of their trunks they have two fingers
They make loud noises, they sound like singers

Elephants are big and strong
And their trunks are very long
They are the largest land mammals
And they are my favourite animals

Elephants like to walk about in mud
They walk about with a *thud!*
They have big ears
Elephants, they're great, let's cheer.

Kirsten McNab (11)
Troon Primary School, Troon

MY FRIEND KATY

My friend Katy is really cool
And fun to hang around with at school.
When I'm sad
She makes me glad
Because she's my friend Katy.

Compared to some
She is a lot of fun.
She'll be my friend
Until the end
'Cause she's my friend Katy.

Katy is always there for me,
Through thick and thin she does see.
The thing that makes her great
Is that nobody does she hate.
That's my friend, kind, caring Katy.

Shona Pollock (11)
Troon Primary School, Troon

FRIENDS

My best friend's name is Seonaid Mann
She lives in a frying pan
Holly is my other friend
Sometimes she drives me round the bend
Wee Steph, she's really small
Compared to others who are tall
Then there's Eilidh, shy and pale
She has a pet bird called Dale

Then there's Hannah, she laughs a lot
When she gets started she can't stop
Kate is clever, she has a pet bunny
Her favourite meal is toast and honey
Kimberly is very crazy
Compared to Hannah, she's very lazy
Suzanne is tallest of the lot
Her brother is a little tot

We're the gang from Barassie Street
Down the town we like to meet
Chips are what we eat
We never frown
Funky friends
You'll never see how close we can be.

Siobhan McCullough (11)
Troon Primary School, Troon

MY SPECIAL DOG

My dog, very cool, I think she rules
She's brown and white with a big brown nose
And she smells like the beach
She eats almost anything
Chicken is what she likes to eat.

She's very, very cute, just like a polar bear
She likes to chew her pork bone which smells really bad
Even though sometimes she gets annoying
I still think she is best.

Ben Colgan (11)
Troon Primary School, Troon

TIGERS!

Tiger, tiger where are you?
I was in the river blue!
Tiger, tiger where have you been?
I've just been in the forest green!

Two big tigers orange and black fur,
They've got big yellow eyes
And they catch the flies.

They sleep in the day
And get up at night,
They sometimes fight.
They stroll about looking for food
And hunt down things that are good.

The little baby cubs jump about
And try to climb the trees,
But sometimes they get stung by the bees.

Tiger, tiger where are you going?
I'm going to do some sewing.
Tiger, tiger, see you later?
Bye-bye, you alligator!

Tanya Peters (11)
Troon Primary School, Troon

THE OCEAN

The ocean deep, blue and alive like us
Twisting and swaying, twisting and swaying, round and round.

Fishes swimming, making no fuss
Going fast through the water, moving without sound.

Deep beneath the ocean lies a sandy floor
Ships just lie there motionless.

Now the ocean is banging on the shore
That's all I can see, nothing less, nothing more.

We must keep the ocean blue and clean
Let the plants live on the beach so more can be planted.

We don't want it polluted and green
Keep it clean and let our wish be granted.

Graeme Birrell (11)
Troon Primary School, Troon

MY DOG

My dog is really small and cute
And likes to chew my ear,
It likes to sit on my knee
And will soon doze off into a dream.

It likes to poo and pee on the carpet,
It's not allowed up on the couch,
Because they are leather.

Christopher King (11)
Troon Primary School, Troon

LIZARDS

Lizards are sometimes brown and green,
Their eyes look dark and very mean,
They like to be in hot places,
Their tails are sometimes skinnier than laces.

If something tries to catch a small lizard by its tail,
The something is surely going to fail,
For the lizard will run, but the tail will stay,
And the tail will grow back on over the days.

Small lizards can run very fast,
It would pass you as quick as a flash,
Small, live insects are what they eat,
They catch them with their long, small feet.

Lizards are sometimes brown and green,
Their eyes are dark and very mean.

Jenny Read (11)
Troon Primary School, Troon

BOYS

I have had it from Heaven to Hell with boys,
They drive me mad with their silly toys.
The clothes they wear, the things they do,
They think they're *so cool!*
Well, they're not! They sit there and call me names,
Then go back to their silly games.
One's called John, one's James,
They're the ones that call me names.
The one called Scott says he's twelve,
I think he is a tot, and believe me I am not.
Oh yeah! - *I hate them! I hate them! I really hate them!*

Jennifer Hendry (10)
Troon Primary School, Troon

SUBSTITUTE TEACHER

A substitute teacher, how terrifying
At this moment I'd rather be crying,
At my desk biting my nails
I feel like I am trapped on rails.

Will she be bossy, will she be kind?
That's just something I'll have to find,
Will her face be like a witch?
Will her eyes give a funny twitch?

Will she have a dotty dress?
Will her feet be a rotten mess?
Will she have a smelly stench?
Or will her legs be baggy and drenched?

I hope she died on the way here
I hope she lost her school career,
Will she be old, will she be young?
Or maybe she'll have a pimpled tongue.

Help!

Kimberley Maxwell (11)
Troon Primary School, Troon

MY BUNNY DUSTY

Dusty bunny you're my honey,
when you run it looks funny.
I was gonna call you my rabbit,
but it only rhymes with crabbit.
You're tiny, sweet and always eat,
and you like to bask in the heat.
My mum and dad love him too,
he's the coolest rabbit you ever knew.
It would be funny if he was blue.

Dusty is black and white
and doesn't bite,
but I wish he wouldn't
put up a fight.
He tries so hard to get away,
when I put him in his hutch each day.
I love my Dusty, he's the best,
better than all the rest!

Kate Wilson (11)
Troon Primary School, Troon

MY POEM ABOUT NOTHING

So here's my poem, it's not very good,
And pizza is one of my favourite foods,
With lots of cheese
I don't like it with peas,
It tastes different from overseas.

My fish is called Splash,
I bought it with my own cash,
It's nice and bold,
And is bright gold.

I've got a little brother called Sam,
He likes sausages in the frying pan,
He's only five and thinks he's big,
And hates being 'it' when playing tig!

So that's my poem for the competition,
I don't think I will win, but that was my mission!

Suzanne Taha (11)
Troon Primary School, Troon

MY BEST BUDDY

Me and my best buddy do everything together,
She says we'll be best friends forever.
Everything I like, she likes the same,
She is so cool, but sometimes a pain.
She's like a sheep, she follows me around,
She is so quiet she doesn't make a sound.
Her hair is dark brown and her eyes big and blue,
Her clothes are funky, they are mostly blue too!

We always agree and never fight,
She keeps my secrets and is always right.
We love to have mud fights and get all muddy
But what I like best about her is that she is my best buddy!

Joanne Welsh (11)
Troon Primary School, Troon

MY FRIENDS

My friend Natalie has carrot hair
She's as small as a bear
She likes to wear
Crop tops and some trousers that flare

My friend Katy is a little pain
She likes the rain
She goes insane
In the rain

My friend Jenny has a fighting brain
She likes to fight
When she sees a pain

But together we make best friends!

Milly White (10)
Troon Primary School, Troon

SWIMMING WITH DOLPHINS

I dream of swimming with dolphins
Gliding through the deep blue sea
Holding on to their fins
As they swim along with me

I dream of swimming with dolphins
Talking to them as we swim
Watching them jump into the night's sky
And it looks as if they can fly

I dream of swimming with dolphins
As we brush by the slippery seaweed
But now it's time to wake up
I wish I could stay forever
But I don't mind, because I will find
The same dolphins in my sleep tonight.

Flora Brown (11)
Troon Primary School, Troon

MY DOG

My dog is very sleepy,
She sleeps all day.
She plays with me all the time,
She's big and cute, it's hard to believe she's mine.
She loves to go to the beach,
Every day we try and teach.

She's black with a wet nose,
She's mental all the time.
I love my dog cos she's mine,
Oh remember, *dogs rule.*

Mathew Morton (11)
Troon Primary School, Troon

MY FAT CAT

My cat Boxer is so fat,
He can eat almost anything,
Especially a rat!
He sometimes gets attacked
By the cat next door,
But Boxer blows his top
And chases him like a wild boar.

Boxer can do a lethal pump
And he is such a lazy lump,
He once did a big jump
And landed on my other cat,
He squashed her like a rat.
When my Mum goes to bed
Boxer follows her to rest his head.

When he wakes up,
He waits to be fed
But my Mum won't get
Out of bed.
Boxer is really cool
And he likes to rule the house!
Boxer is so cute and chubby
But sadly he doesn't have a hubby.
If you saw him, you would love him
He is *simply the best!*

Boxer!

Rory McGee (11)
Troon Primary School, Troon

MY DOG SAM

My dog Sam is really clever he
    can roll over
for his treats and gives me
    his paws

Sam is really cool
    when I go
into a shop Sam barks
    his head off
because he doesn't like
    to be left alone

Sam can be let off
    the lead
he comes back for
    more fun

Sam is scared of
    my friend
Jennifer, I don't
    know why

He likes my other
    friends Milly
Katy and Shona too

Sam is the *best!*

Natalie Harding (11)
Troon Primary School, Troon

FAT PAT

Once there was a man called Pat,
He ate too much and got fat.
Food he ate morning, noon and night,
Pat looked a right sight.
He sat in his house eating cakes,
Never going out with his mates.
He loved curries and pies,
The best are from McKies.
People told him to stop eating food,
He said he would
But he didn't diet and didn't trust his mate,
So he just ate and ate.
Here's a warning, 'Don't eat as much food as Pat
Because he died young 'cause he was fat'.

Ewan Murray (11)
Troon Primary School, Troon

THE WEDDING

We're going to a wedding
That we're really dreading
With lots of practical jokes
We'll bring water balloons
Filled to the rim
Loads of fake spiders
Invisible string
Cap guns
Whoopee cushions
And other jokes too
We'll enjoy this wedding
We hope you do too.

Jamie Watson (10)
Troon Primary School, Troon

I FEEL SICK

Set before school sick
I wish I wasn't work sick
I wish I wasn't dinner sick

I feel sick

Cheese makes me feel sick
Egg makes me feel sick
I wish I wasn't food sick

I feel sick

My dog makes me feel sick
My rat makes me feel sick
I wish I wasn't pet sick

I feel sick

Mark Auld (11)
Troon Primary School, Troon

RUGBY

R   ugby is a very messy sport,
U   gly people play in the scrum,
G   et all muddy on your arms and legs,
B   all is like an egg and bounces all over the place,
Y   ou get a try if you are good at rugby.

Allstair Wright (11)
Troon Primary School, Troon

HIDDEN TREASURES

Deep far down in the deep blue sea,
Lies a secret to be kept between you and me,
It's gold and shiny
And waiting to be found,
We have to go now,
No time to hang around.

We have to start our exploration,
Once we're finished we will be known
Throughout the nation,
Now we have to pack,
Don't forget a snack,
I hope you don't get seasick,
Come on, we need to get there quick.

We have to go quite far,
All the journey without a car,
The whole journey is by ship,
We can't stop for a dip,
The plans that I drew,
So we know what to do.

Now we have set sail,
We shall have piles of fan mail,
Now it won't be long,
It should not go wrong,
If you would like to measure,
Yes, you have got it,
Not far to the treasure.

Alastair Dewar (11)
Troon Primary School, Troon

SWIMMING

When swimming through the swimming pool
Oh how this water's very cool.
I wish I was swimming for school
When my friends are shouting, 'She rules.'

I love to dive and jump in the pool
When it is very cool.
I slide down the slide and shout, 'Hooray!'
And wonder is this better than to play?

There's Shona, Natalie, Jennifer and Milly too
They come in and swim too.
They are all good swimmers
And all fun too.

I glide through the pool
Will all my friends
We much around going round the bends.

We get out of the pool
To get our food
I remember I forgot my food
Then to my surprise I see a splash.

The splash was made by a man
Then I realise swimming is real cool.

Katy McMillan (11)
Troon Primary School, Troon